CHARLESTON
classic
DESSERTS

CHARLESTON *classic* DESSERTS

Recipes from
Favorite Restaurants

JANICE SHAY

Foreword by Marion Sullivan

Photography by Deborah Whitlaw Llewellyn

PELICAN PUBLISHING COMPANY
Gretna 2008

The word "Pelican" and the depiction of a pelican are trademarks
of Pelican Publishing Company, Inc., and are registered in the
U.S. Patent and Trademark Office.
ISBN-13: 978-1-58980-545-3

Edited by Andrea Chesman, Molly Hall Nagy, Judy Arvites, and Joanna Brodmann

Photograph of Vacherin, page 88, reprinted with permission; © Terry Manier

Layout based on a design by Kit Wohl

Printed in Singapore

Published by Pelican Publishing Company, Inc.
1000 Burmaster Street, Gretna, Louisiana 70053

For my sweet husband Patrick.

CONTENTS

Chapter 4   CUSTARDS & PUDDINGS

Chapter 5   ICE CREAM, GELATO, COOKIES, & SAUCES

FOREWORD

It's no secret that the Southerners are known for their desserts, and Charlestonians are no exception. As far back as 1847, *The Carolina Housewife*, written by a Lady of Charleston, lists some one hundred and eighty recipes for sweets ranging from the humble corn cake to the French fancy, Charlotte Russe. That the identity of the authors proved to be Sarah Rutledge, daughter of Edward Rutledge, and Henrietta Middleton Rutledge, sister of Arthur Middleton, both men signers of the Declaration of Independence, ensures the value this book will always hold historically.

Many of the desserts in *The Carolina Housewife* are clearly European in origin: blancmange, trifle, tea cakes, ginger cakes and puddings. Sweets that we consider sophisticated, such as puff pastry and Bavarian Cream, can be found within its pages, as can directions for that current rage, crème brûlée, titled by the Rutledges' "Burnt Cream." "Pour boiled custard into a dish," it reads; "when cold, grate sugar over it, and brown it with a salamander or a hot shovel." Who knew!

There are baked bread puddings: Poor Man's Bread Pudding, in which the bread is soaked in water, sweetened, seasoned and baked, and Bread and Butter Pudding, in which the bread is buttered, then layered with a "rich custard" and citron and baked. There's pound cake in the traditional pound of butter, pound of sugar, pound of flour ratio. You'll find ice creams, as well as sorbets, which are called "sherbets," made from lemon, strawberry, pineapple, blackberry, and peach.

Other flavors that are evident tell us more about Charleston's history. Apples, figs, and raisins are sprinkled throughout. Coconuts, coming in to the thriving port from Cuba with bananas, show up in several recipes. Oranges are in many. Oranges and lemons were grown locally. In fact, an orange grove once flourished inside the city, occasioning the name Orange Street. Orange trees can be found bearing here today, as do Meyer lemons and kefir limes, which prosper when planted in Charleston gardens and in pots on sunny piazzas.

And rice, the particular crop of Carolina Gold unique to the Low Country, which created its wealthy society of Charleston planters, abounds in desserts as well as savories. It's hard to imagine a recipe that showcases its delicate beauty better than rice pudding, and the one included in this book is better than any I have ever tasted.

South Carolina's Anson Mills is reintroducing Carolina Gold Rice back into the market. If you want to capture the essence of a true classic Charleston dessert, purchase half a pound and experience history when you make this rice pudding.

Charleston Receipts, published by the Junior League of Charleston in 1950, and presently in its thirtieth edition, gives a look into the kitchens of Charleston households in "modern" days. In a city where tradition is revered, it is not surprising that many of the same desserts can still be found, albeit with updated cooking instructions. Here still are the puddings, pones, ice creams and syllabub, and several versions of the ever-popular Charlotte Russe.

Chocolate, which was featured in only one dessert in *The Carolina Housewife*, is seen in *Charleston Receipts* to have firmly captured the Charleston sweet tooth, as evidenced in chocolate pots de crème, soufflé, meringue pie, fudge, brownies, and multiple cakes. Pecans, too, have become part of the dessert vernacular. Though not indigenous to South Carolina, pecan trees are now part of the landscape, and pecan pie a part of the dessert menu.

In *Charleston Receipts* we also find the recipe for the much-misinterpreted Huguenot Torte. As Charleston had an influx of French Huguenot settlers in the mid-eighteenth century, legend has attributed this dessert to be of French Huguenot origin. Not so. It's origins trace back to Ozark pudding and its name to the Huguenot Tavern, popular in Charleston in the mid-twentieth century, where it was served.

Today, we have it all. Here in Charleston, we are still making our favorite desserts from *Charleston Receipts,* but we are also luxuriating in the selection of sumptuous offerings available in our sophisticated culinary scene. Talented pastry chefs, chefs, caterers, and bakers are reinterpreting old classics and inventing new ways to carry forward traditional Charleston flavors. In their creativity you will observe elements of respect, humor, imagination, and fabulous flair. It is, as you will see in this book, the best of times for those of us who love the many creations of the sweet kitchen.

—Marion Sullivan
Culinary Institute of Charleston Program Specialist, Charleston Magazine *Food Editor, food and travel writer*

INTRODUCTION

"The proof of the pudding is in the eating." —Old English proverb

Charleston, South Carolina, attracts hundreds of thousands of tourists annually with its rich history and languid Southern beauty. It is a city of firsts—the Charleston Museum is the oldest in the country; Dock Street Theater, which opened in 1736, was one of the first theaters in the states; a 1770 statue of William Pitt is the first commemorating a public figure in America; the first shots of the Civil War were fired at Fort Sumter; the first Spoleto Festival U.S.A. was held in 1977.

Yes, history abounds in Charleston, but it is only part of what keeps people returning to this lovely city by the sea. The gracious manners of the locals, the vibrant art community, the plethora of stores, museums, and schools, the walkability of a downtown that is as beautiful as any in the country, and always, the great food—these are more of the jewels in Charleston's crown.

The food in Charleston is simply divine. The restaurateurs are commited to using local ingredients, and serving many of the freshest and most exciting dishes in the South. Their menus are varied and impressive, and they always feature desserts that are stand-outs. When I started researching this book, I had the mistaken impression that classic dishes were hard to find. I was wrong. The local chefs have taken classic tastes and flavors and updated them, yes—but the memories are still there. Mike Lata's Rice Pudding is the best you'll find, and it is a recipe as old as the city and the Carolina Gold rice fields that inspired it; Mitchell Crosby's Charleston Trifle would be at home on any Victorian table, and is a thing of beauty; and the cakes, pies, cobblers and puddings in this book offer wonderful new twists on standard recipes handed down for generations.

I am always pleased to meet a pastry chef. As a rule, they are the happiest cooks in the kitchen—their food puts a smile on any face, and the dish is almost never returned untouched. Can you think of a time that you blamed a case of indigestion on a dessert? No. It is always the fault of the tomato sauce, or the spicy sausage—never the chocolate pudding! Thanks to all the talented local chefs who shared their joy in the kitchen. It made my work in putting together a book of dessert recipes—choosing, tasting, photographing, listening and learning their history and method—very happy work, indeed.

Finally, I am reminded of the proverb that is often misquoted, but whose true meaning is so pertinent to this cookbook. The proof is not, as we sometimes think, "in the pudding". The proof of the pudding is in the eating, which means that the true value or quality of something can only be judged when it's put to use. I hope that this cookbook will prove to be useful, and will bring you many hours of enjoyable cooking and fabulous eating!

Janice Shay
October, 2007

CAKES & SOUFFLÉS

There is a longstanding tradition of serving puddings and custards for dessert in Charleston, so it is not surprising that chefs have consistently kept them on local menus. What is surprising—or at least happily note-worthy—is that each of these desserts offers a new and innovative twist to an old recipe.

Modern Charleston chefs use creative combinations of tastes to update a classic dish—figs served with Carolina Gold rice pudding, sweet biscuits with orange custard sauce, and red velvet bread pudding are a few of the standouts that come to mind. Puddings may harken back to our childhood days, but these innovations also serve to satisfy our more sophisticated palates.

Carolina's is housed in a Revolutionary era building, less than 100 feet from the Cooper River. Charleston native Chef Jeremiah Bacon stays true to classic Southern traditions, and is the creative force behind the wonderful food served here. He was on CBS' The Early Show this summer, during which he cooked along the windy Battery with host Harry Smith.

For the first time in 100 years, Carolina Gold Rice was grown in the region at Kensington Plantation with a first yield in 2007. Richard Stoney, owner of the plantation, plans to supply his restaurant Carolina's with the harvest from this historic crop. Several heirloom rice crops, along with spices and vegetables are being cultivated on Kensington, all to be served at the oldest fine dining establishment in Charleston.

A debut dinner was held at the James Beard House in New York this year, with figs, collard greens, mixed greens, red peppers, black-eyed peas and spices from the garden. Chef Jeremiah Bacon calls it "culinary storytelling," with the history of Charleston told in the classic food of the region.

CAROLINA'S RESTAURANT
ALMOND POUND CAKE WITH SMOKED HONEY ICE CREAM

Simple is sometimes best, and it doesn't get any better than this moist, lovely pound cake.

SERVES 8 TO 10

2 1/2 sticks unsalted butter, at room
  temperature
1/2 vanilla bean
1 1/3 cups sugar
3 large eggs
3 large egg yolks
1 1/2 tablespoons water

1/2 teaspoon salt
1 cup all-purpose flour
1/2 cup almond flour

For SMOKED HONEY ICE CREAM recipe,
see page 90

Preheat the oven to 325° F.

Line a 9-inch by 5-inch loaf pan with parchment paper.

Beat the butter in an electric mixer fitted with a paddle attachment until smooth and shiny, about 15 seconds. Add the vanilla bean to the sugar. Sprinkle the sugar slowly over the butter and beat the mixture until light, fluffy, and almost white, about 5 minutes, scraping down the bowl frequently.

Stir together the eggs, egg yolks, and water until well combined. Slowly add to the butter mixture in slow, thin stream, beating well. Beat in the salt.

Combine the two flours in a bowl. Sift one-third of flour mixture over the batter and fold in. Repeat two more times until all the flour is incorporated. Pour the batter into the prepared pan.

Bake for about 1 hour, rotating the pan after 30 minutes. The cake is done when a tester inserted near the center of a cake comes out clean.

Cool on wire rack for 10 minutes. Remove the cake from the pan and cool completely.

MIDDLETON PLACE
HUGUENOT TORTE

Huguenot Torte is a Charleston favorite since the early 20th century. It is believed to have been first served at the Huguenot Tavern in Charleston during the 1930s, and is an adaptation of a dish from Arkansas called Ozark Pudding.

SERVES 8

4 large eggs
3 cups sugar
1/2 cup all-purpose flour
5 teaspoons baking powder
1/2 teaspoon salt
2 cups chopped tart cooking apples, such as
   Granny Smiths

2 cups pecans, chopped
2 teaspoons vanilla extract

Whipped cream, to serve
sprig of ming, to garnish

Preheat the oven to 325° F. Butter two 8-inch by 12-inch baking pans.

Beat the eggs and sugar in an electric mixer with a wire whip attachment until very frothy and lemon-colored. Mix in the flour, baking powder, salt, apples, pecans, and vanilla. Pour into the prepared baking pans.

Bake for about 45 minutes, or until crusty and brown, rotating the pans halfway through baking. (Baking in a convection oven will cut the baking time by half, give or take a few minutes.)

Allow to cool to just over room temperature before serving. To serve, slip a spatula under each torte and slide onto a plate. Cover with a dollop of whipped cream. Using two spatulas, one for getting the torte out of the pan, the other for getting the torte to release from the pan, may make getting the torte out of the pan easier.

Middleton Place is an 18th-century rice plantation that's now a National Historic Landmark. The estate is home to sixty-five acres of formal landscaped gardens, and one of the South's most romantic inns. The Restaurant on the grounds was among the Top 10 restaurants chosen by American Way Magazine *for its authentic regional cuisine.*

The Middleton Place Restaurant evolved from a 1928 fundraiser held by the Junior League of Charleston, who set up a spring season Tea Room in the Rice Mill. The League volunteers used an upstairs kitchen to prepare okra soup and sandwiches for garden visitors. The Tea Room was moved to a former guesthouse on the plantation in 1949, where the restaurant now stands.

Many of its recipes were developed by renowned Southern Chef Edna Lewis, and includes Low Country favorites like Hoppin' John, okra jumbo and she-crab soup. The fresh ingredients are harvested right from the plantation's garden. The restaurant belongs to Slow Food Charleston, a group that promotes locally grown, sustainable foods.

Walking the lovely gardens, touring the plantation, and eating some of Middleton Place Restaurant's fine cuisine is a rare treat and shouldn't be missed.

LANA RESTAURANT AND BAR
STICKY FIG CAKE WITH ALMOND GELATO

SERVES 12

CAKE

1/2 cup unsalted butter, at room temperature
1 cup firmly packed light brown sugar
3 large eggs
1/2 teaspoon ground cinnamon
1 cup chopped dried figs
1 1/4 cups boiling water
1 teaspoon baking soda
2 cups self-rising flour

GLAZE

3/4 cup dark muscovado or Barbados sugar
6 tablespoon unsalted butter
1/4 cup heavy cream

ALMOND GELATO

3/4 cup almonds, processed (see below)
2 tablespoons almond paste
3 cups milk
1 cup heavy cream
5 large egg yolks
3/4 cup granulated white sugar
1 teaspoon vanilla extract

See page 92 for Caramel Sauce

It was originally called Cafe Lana when it operated on Cumberland Street. But when Chef-owner Drazen Romic was faced with moving, it meant a larger space in the Crosstown area and a new partner in Chef John Ondo. Lana is the new, more expansive incarnation, but still bears the name of Romic's daughter.

Native Charlestonian Ondo had cooked in other local restaurants, and brings a straightforward style to Lana that means seeking out the best ingredients, and not overdoing the preparation. Ondo's no-nonsense attitude won him press as one of the four "Hottest Chefs" in Charleston in the City Paper. In the Crosstown area, it's become a neighborhood favorite and its loyal patronage is growing through word of mouth.

It's a causal, intimate setting that's also a showcase of local art, with rotating works on view. The menu is inspired by southern Europe, but each dish maintains a regional essence rather than going for Euro-fusion cuisine. A perfect example is the pairing of figs and almonds in the scrumptious dessert featured here.

Preheat the oven to 350° F. Grease a 9-inch springform pan.

TO MAKE THE CAKE, combine the butter and brown sugar in an electric mixer fitted with a paddle attachment. Beat at medium speed until fluffy, about 4 minutes. Add the eggs, one at a time, beating well after each addition and scraping down the bowl. Beat in the cinnamon.

Combine the figs and boiling water in a bowl, cover, and let steep for 5 minutes. Add the baking soda and puree in a blender.

Add the flour to the butter mixture, then add the pureed figs and mix until well combined. Pour into the prepared pan. Bake for 45 minutes, or until a tester inserted near the center comes out clean. Cool on a wire rack for 30 minutes, then remove from pan and glaze.

TO MAKE THE GLAZE, combine the muscovado sugar, butter, and cream in a heavy saucepan. Simmer for 3 minutes. Pour directly over the fig cake.

TO MAKE THE GELATO, pulse the almonds and almond paste in a food processor until broken into little pieces. Combine the milk, cream, and nut mixture in a saucepan and bring to a simmer.

In another bowl, beat the egg yolks and white sugar until pale. Slowly pour a little of the hot cream mixture into the yolk mixture. Continue to whisk in small amounts of milk at a time until the temperatures of the two mixtures are equal. Whisk the yolk mixture into the cream mixture. Cook over medium heat, stirring, until the mixture has thickened and will coat the back of the spoon. Remove from the heat and stir in the vanilla. Transfer to a bowl. Place the bowl in a larger bowl of ice and let cool, stirring occasionally.

Transfer to an ice-cream maker and freeze according to the manufacturer's directions.

TO SERVE, slice the cake and place on a plate. Top each serving with a scoop of the gelato.

ANGELFISH CAKE BAKERY
SHERRY PETITS FOURS

These little beauties are almost too precious to eat, but I'll bet that the yield of 40 will actually only feed 8 people. They taste every bit as good as they look!

MAKES 40

CAKE

2 1/4 cups unsalted butter, at room temperature
3 cups granulated white sugar
1 cup sour cream, at room temperature
1/2 cup good-quality Sherry
3 cups all-purpose flour
1/3 cup cornstarch
1 teaspoon kosher salt
1 teaspoon baking soda
8 large eggs at room temperature

GLAZE

1/2 cup unsalted butter, melted
2/3 cup good-quality Sherry
4 cups confectioners' sugar

Sprinkles or flowers, to decorate

Angelfish Cake is the paired-down, simplified essence of previous restaurant endeavors of the mother-daughter team of Chris and Jennifer Thomas. For many years, the two ran AngelFish, a James Island eatery with vegetarian fare and scrumptious desserts.

This is a family of restaurateurs—Chris' mother Lucy ran Stella's Spaghetti in the 1940s, and Evangeline in downtown Charleston. With her father and brother Michael, Chris opened Momma's Money on upper King, before opening her own diner-style restaurant called King Street Eden. Chris and daughter Jennifer ran the Sun Spot on Folly beach before opening the original AngelFish, and both featured their signature vegetarian fare.

Now they have a storefront selling sandwiches and desserts, with much of the business coming from catering, and their cakes and pies are always in demand. They have catered for many loyal local clients for 20 years.

Preheat the oven to 350° F. Butter and flour an 18-inch by 12-inch pan.

To MAKE THE CAKE, combine the butter and white sugar in an electric mixer fitted with a paddle attachment. Beat at high speed until fluffy. Decrease the speed and add the eggs, two at a time, beating well after each addition and scraping down the bowl. Add the sour cream and Sherry and beat until well combined.

Sift together the flour, cornstarch, kosher salt, and baking soda. Turn the mixer to low, and add the flour mixture, beating just to combine. Pour into the prepared pan. Smooth out with a spatula.

Bake the cake for 30 minutes, until a tester inserted near the center comes out clean.

Cool the cake thoroughly and chill in the refrigerator to firm up

To MAKE THE GLAZE, combine the melted butter, sherry, and confectioners' sugar. Beat until completely smooth.

When the cake is completely cold, cut into 1-inch squares using a wooden ruler. Place the cake squares on a rack set over waxed paper, to catch drips. Spoon the glaze over the cake squares and let set. They may require two coats to cover evenly. Decorate with sprinkles or flowers.

the square onion

The name of this deli comes from its location in a Mt. Pleasant neighborhood, being on the "square on I'On". Across the harbor from Charleston, I'On is an award-winning 243-acre development that's called neo-traditional because of its shared green spaces and pedestrian-friendly walkways.

Mary and Cary Zapatka opened Square Onion in 2001 out of a belief in homemade food, and the tradition of eating together as a family. Mary had been general manager of Magnolias restaurant for a dozen years, and Cary was with the Boathouse, helping them open their first location.

Many of the Square Onion's recipes were passed down from mothers and grandparents on both sides. The Zapatkas are big believers in the dinner table as a place to nurture the family, especially kids, and have many take-out meals ready to sit down and enjoy together.

It's excellent Southern comfort food, with favorites like the hamburger tater tot casserole and caramel cake, an old family recipe. Sitting with others at the big wooden table in the front of the deli feels delightfully like eating at your mom's kitchen table.

SQUARE ONION CAFE
SILVER MOON CARAMEL CAKE

This recipe was owner Mary Zapatka's great grandmother's recipe. It was named by Mary's dad when he was just a small boy.

SERVES 10

CAKE

3 cups sifted all-purpose flour
1 tablespoon baking powder
1/2 teaspoon salt
4 large eggs, separated
1 cup unsalted butter, at room temperature
2 cups sugar
2 teaspoons vanilla extract
1 cup milk

SILVER MOON FROSTING

1 1/2 cups unsalted butter
4 1/2 cups sugar
1 1/2 cups milk
1 tablespoon vanilla extract

Preheat the oven to 350°F. Butter and flour three 10-inch cake pans.

To make the cake, sift the flour, baking powder, and salt together 3 times. Set aside.

Beat the egg whites in a clean bowl until stiff but not dry peaks form.

Cream the butter in an electric mixer with a paddle attachment until light. Gradually add the sugar, beating until light and fluffy. Add the egg yolks, one at a time, beating well after each addition and scraping down the bowl. Alternately add the dry ingredients and milk, one third at a time. Beat until smooth after each addition. Add the vanilla. Fold in the egg whites. Divide the batter among the prepared pans.

Bake for 25 to 30 minutes, until a tester inserted near the center comes out clean.

Cool on wire racks for 10 minutes. Remove the pans and continue cooling the cake layers.

To make the frosting, combine the butter, sugar, and milk in 4-quart or larger saucepan. Bring to a boil and cook, stirring constantly, to the softball stage (220° F on a candy thermometer). Remove from heat and beat at medium-high speed until the sheen dulls and the frosting is of spreading consistency. Add the vanilla after beating a couple of minutes. Care should be taken while beating because the frosting is very hot. Do not beat too long or the frosting will harden. If the frosting becomes too stiff, beat in a little milk, 1 tablespoon at a time, to bring it back to spreading consistency. Work quickly when spreading on the cake or the frosting will set before the cake is covered.

HIGH COTTON
PRALINE SOUFFLÉ

A soufflé is often referred to as the "dessert of kings" and this one, with its distinctive praline flavor, is certainly worthy of the title.

SERVES 6

SOUFFLÉ BASE

2 tablespoons heavy cream

2 tablespoons milk

1/2 cup firmly packed brown sugar

2 egg yolks

1 tablespoon all-purpose flour

1/4 cup pecans, toasted

2 tablespoons molasses

MERINGUE

2 cups egg whites (approximately 9 egg whites)

2 cups granulated sugar

1/2 teaspoon crème tartar

CHOCOLATE SAUCE

1 cup heavy whipping cream

4 ounces milk chocolate

4 ounces dark chocolate

Preheat the oven to 375° F.

Lightly butter six 6- to 8-ounce ramekins with softened butter. Divide about 1 cup granulated white sugar among the ramekins. Roll the sugar in the ramekins until they are well coated with sugar. Dump out any excess sugar.

Combine the milk, cream, and 1/4 cup of the brown sugar in a small, heavy saucepan. Bring almost to a boil.

Beat the egg yolks with the remaining 1/4 cup brown sugar in a medium bowl until well combined. Sift the flour over the mixture and blend in until the mixture is as smooth as possible. Slowly pour the hot cream mixture into the yolks. Return to the stove over medium heat and cook, stirring constantly, until thickened. Add the pecans and molasses. Cook for 30 seconds more.

Place the saucepan in a bowl filled with ice and chill, stirring occasionally.

FOR THE MERINGUE, combine the egg whites and cream of tartar in an electric mixer fitted with a whip attachment. Beat until soft peaks form. Gradually add the white sugar, beating until the mixture forms stiff peaks.

In a separate bowl, combine the chilled egg yolk mixture with about one-quarter of the whipped egg whites. Mix vigorously. Slowly fold the rest of the egg whites into the mixture. Spoon the soufflé mixture into the prepared ramekins.

Bake for about 10 minutes, until the soufflé rises and the top is golden.

FOR THE SAUCE, melt chocolates in either a double boiler, or in a stainless bowl, set over a pot of simmering water. Slowly whisk in cream and set aside. Pour into a small pitcher or serving dish to be used at table to spoon over finished soufflés.

TO SERVE, sprinkle with the confectioners' sugar, drizzle with chocolate sauce and serve immediately.

Everything about High Cotton promises comfortable luxury, and reflects its name, an old Southern plantation reference to livin' large. Tropical palm fans slowly move the breeze in a room with heart-pine floors and high ceilings. The ambience is fresh and refined, and the interior has the masculine feel of the home of a wealthy gentleman farmer.

Opened in 1999 with a menu designed by Chef Frank Lee, it's a decidedly hearty line-up of Carolina game, steak, and seasonal seafood. It's been called a Southern-style steakhouse, but this would be the antebellum version, where planters might gather to toast a good crop.

High Cotton has multiple dining rooms, and a bar with music, making it a perfect place to spend a slow, indulgent afternoon or evening. Good food, great atmosphere, and a feeling of old Charleston— go and enjoy!

The cool elegance of Cypress's interior belies the excitement and energy that their food demonstrates. Cypress won Best New Restaurant in 2001 from Esquire Magazine. The circa 1834 historic building has exposed brick walls and soaring multi-story heights, with added contemporary elements of glass and steel.

A visually dazzling three-story wine wall holds thousands of labels, mostly California and French varieties. Cypress holds the Award of Excellence for its wine selection from Wine Spectator.

Chef Donald Barickman's cuisine is Lowcountry with innovation, like the recipe featured here. Pastry Chef Kelly Wilson says this is one of her favorites because it marries the tastes of a classical French dessert with Low Country flavors.

This trendy restaurant is sophisticated and fun. I always expect to see a line of paparazzi waiting outside, but, happily, the food is always the star at Cypress.

CYPRESS
PECAN BROWN BUTTER FINANCIERS

SERVES 6

FINANCIERS

1 cup unsalted butter
2/3 cup pecans
1 1/2 cups confectioners' sugar
1/2 cup all-purpose flour
2 teaspoons baking powder
Pinch of salt
5 egg whites, at room temperature
1 1/2 teaspoons vanilla extract

For CARAMEL PARFAIT recipe, see page 93

BOURBON MOUSSELINE

2 tablespoons light brown sugar
3 large egg yolks
3 tablespoons bourbon
3/4 cup heavy cream
1/4 vanilla bean, split and scraped

BOURBON MACERATED GRANNY SMITH APPLE

2 Granny Smith apples, peeled, cored, and finely diced
1/2 cup granulated white sugar
Pinch of salt
1/4 vanilla bean, split and scraped
1/4 cup bourbon
Apple cider

TO MAKE THE FINANCIERS, melt the butter in a heavy saucepan over medium heat. Cook until the solids in the butter begin to brown and the butter smells nutty. Pour the brown butter into a bowl and set aside to cool at room temperature.

Prepare six (5-ounce) ramekins by generously coating them with softened butter, paying special attention to the bottom corners. Dust the buttered ramekins with flour and tap out the excess. Place the prepared ramekins on a sheet pan.

Pulse the pecans in a food processor until almost finely ground, stopping before they begin to clump. Add the confectioners' sugar and process for 30 seconds, or until thoroughly combined.

Sift together the flour, baking powder, and salt. Add to the mixture in the food processor and process until combined. Transfer to a large bowl.

Combine the egg whites and vanilla in a mixing bowl until well blended. Fold into the dry ingredients. Measure out 11 tablespoons (5 1/2 fluid ounces) of the cooled, but still liquid brown butter and stir into the batter (any remaining brown butter can be reserved for later use). Divide the batter among the prepared ramekins.

Cover the ramekins and place in the refrigerator. It is preferable for the batter to rest overnight, but, if necessary, the financiers can be baked after 3 hours of chilling.

Preheat the oven to 350° F.

With the ramekins still on the sheet pan, bake for 15 minutes. Rotate the sheet pan and bake an additional 10 to 15 minutes, until the cakes are a shade past golden and still slightly spongy in the center.

Remove from the oven. Immediately unmold the financiers onto a clean countertop or sheet of parchment paper, using a thin bladed knife to loosen the sides of any stubborn cakes from the ramekins.

Serve immediately or cool completely, and store refrigerated. Reheat prior to serving.

TO MAKE THE BOURBON MOUSSELINE, whisk together the brown sugar, egg yolks, and bourbon in

a large stainless steel bowl set over a pot of boiling water. Whisk the mixture over medium heat until completely foamy and hot to the touch. Be careful not to overcook, or you will curdle the egg yolks.

Transfer the bowl to an ice bath and whisk continuously until cool.

Whip the cream and vanilla seeds to medium peaks.

When the egg mixture is cool, whisk in whipped cream. Chill until needed. This keeps for up to 3 days. If the mousseline loses its fluffiness during this time, it can be rewhipped.

TO PREPARE THE MACERATED APPLES, combine the apples, white sugar, salt, vanilla seeds, and bourbon in a heavy saucepan. Add enough apple cider to completely cover the apples. Bring to a slow boil over low heat. Simmer the apples, stirring gently and intermittently, until the apples become transparent, approximately 10 minutes

Remove from the heat. Transfer the apples and cooking liquid to a stainless steel bowl. Place the bowl in an ice bath and cool the apples completely. Drain off the liquid before serving.

TO ASSEMBLE THE DESSERT, place 2 tablespoons of bourbon mousseline on each plate. Top with a warm financier. Sprinkle a tablespoon or so of drained macerated apple over each cake. Place a scoop of caramel parfait atop the financier and serve.

NOTE: Optional accompaniments include ground candied pecans and dried apple chips.

LEMON BUTTERMILK POUND CAKE WITH BERRIES AND HONEY PARFAIT

This is a nice, light summer dessert, highlighted by the fresh, local berries.

SERVES 4 TO 6

LEMON BUTTERMILK POUND CAKE

6 tablespoons unsalted butter, at room
    temperature
3/4 cup sugar
Zest of 2 lemons, finely grated
3 large eggs
2 cups all-purpose flour
1 1/2 teaspoons baking powder
1/8 teaspoon baking soda
1/2 teaspoon salt
1/2 cup buttermilk
Juice of 1 lemon

LAVENDER SIMPLE SYRUP

1/2 cup sugar
1/2 cup water
1 tablespoon dried lavender flowers

HONEY FROZEN PARFAIT

2 cups heavy cream
1 teaspoon plain gelatin
2 tablespoons cold water
4 large egg yolks
1/3 cup honey
Pinch of salt
1/2 vanilla bean

Fresh berries (raspberries, blackberries,
    strawberries, blueberries), to serve
Fresh lavender sprigs, to garnish

Preheat the oven to 350° F. Grease a 9-inch by 5-inch loaf pan.

TO MAKE THE CAKE, combine the butter, sugar, and lemon zest in an electric mixer with a paddle attachment. Beat together until fluffy. Add the eggs, one at a time, beating just until combined after each addition. Scrape down the bowl and beat for 1 more minute.

Sift together the flour, baking powder, baking soda, and salt in a medium bowl. In a second bowl, combine the buttermilk and lemon juice.

Add the flour mixture to the egg mixture in two parts, alternating with the buttermilk mixture. Pour the batter into the prepared pan.

Bake for 20 minutes, then rotate the pan, and continue baking for another 20 minutes, until a tester inserted near the center of the cake comes out clean.

Cool the cake in the pan for 10 minutes. Unmold and allow the cake to cool completely on a wire rack.

TO MAKE THE LAVENDER SYRUP, combine the sugar, water, and lavender in a nonreactive pan. Bring to a boil, stirring to dissolve the sugar. Remove from the heat. Steep for a minimum of 30 minutes. Strain and chill until needed.

TO MAKE THE FROZEN PARFAIT, whip the cream to soft peaks.

Sprinkle the gelatin over the cold water and stir to combine.

Combine the egg yolks, honey, and salt in a stainless steel bowl. Scrape the vanilla seeds into the mixture. Set the bowl over a pan of simmering water and cook over medium heat flame until the mixture has thickened and is lighter in color. Remove from the heat and let cool, stirring occasionally.

Melt the softened gelatin in a microwave at half power in five second intervals until completely liquid and whisk it into the still-warm yolk-honey mixture. Allow this parfait base to cool to room temperature.

Fold the whipped cream into the cream mixture before the gelatin sets. Start with a third of the cream to lighten the parfait base, then fold in the remaining whipped cream. Cover tightly and freeze overnight.

TO SERVE, slice the pound cake. Toss the berries with enough lavender syrup to coat. Spoon berries onto each plate. Top the berries with pound cake. Scoop the honey parfait and place on the plates. Garnish with sprigs of fresh lavender, if desired.

Situated inside the Sanctuary Resort at Kiawah Island, the Ocean Room is an elegant restaurant with views of the South Carolina coastline. It's been awarded the Mobil 4 Star, the AAA 4 Diamond rating, and Wine Spectator's Award of Excellence.

Guests to the Ocean Room walk through wrought-iron gates designed by Savannah blacksmith John Boyd Smith, with Lowcountry motifs of egrets, sea grass and sea oats. There are two private dining rooms, one overlooking the greens and ocean, the other named the Wine Room, with a walnut floor and mahogany wine racks.

The cuisine draws inspiration from Spain, southern France, Italy and northern Africa. Pastry Chef Carrie Chapman, formerly of Woodlands Resort and Inn, draws on classical French training and a girlhood dream to be a chef. She made her first dessert—a bright pink birthday cake—at age six. Her grandmother made wedding cakes, and inspired her to pursue a career as a pastry chef.

The Ocean Room was named restaurant of the year by the Charleston Post and Courier.

KIAWAH RESORT
CHOCOLATE KEY LIME CAKE

SERVES 12

CHOCOLATE SPONGE CAKE

6 large egg yolks
8 large whole eggs
1 2/3 cups sugar
1 cup all-purpose flour
1 cup unsweetened cocoa powder
8 large egg whites
2/3 cup sugar
Pinch of cream of tartar

KEY LIME MOUSSE

2 teaspoons unflavored gelatin
1 tablespoon cold water
2/3 cup whole milk
7 tablespoons Key lime juice
4 large egg yolks
1/3 cup sugar
3/4 cup heavy cream

RASPBERRY MOUSSE

2 teaspoons unflavored gelatin
1/2 cup raspberry puree.
4 large egg yolks
3 tablespoons sugar
3/4 cup heavy cream

COCOA SAUCE

1 cup cocoa
1 cup sugar
Pinch of salt
1 cup water

GARNISH

Fresh raspberries
Chocolate curls

Preheat the oven to 400° F. Coat two half-sheet pans with nonstick spray and line the pans with parchment paper.

To make the cake, combine the egg yolks, whole eggs, and sugar in an electric mixer with a wire whip attachment. Beat at high speed until the batter falls in ribbons when the beaters are lifted.

Sift the flour and cocoa together and gradually fold into the egg mixture.

In a clean, dry bowl, beat the whites with a third of the sugar and the cream of tartar until foamy. Add the remaining sugar and beat until stiff peaks form. Fold the whites into the egg-flour mixture in three batches. Divide the batter between two prepared pans.

Bake the two half sheet pans on two separate racks that are located towards the middle of the oven. Bake the cakes for 10 minutes and then rotate them and bake 10 minutes more, or until the cake springs back to the touch.

Cool on wire racks. Once the cakes are cooled, gently remove the "skin" from the surface of the cake, by using a serrated knife. This will ensure that the mousse sticks to the cake.

To make the Key lime mousse, sprinkle the gelatin over the water in a small bowl to soften.

Combine the milk and key lime juice in a small saucepan and bring to a gentle boil. Combine the egg yolks and sugar in a small bowl and whisk until well combined. Pour a small amount of the hot milk mixture into the yolk mixture and stir well to temper the eggs. Immediately stir the egg yolk mixture into the saucepan and cook, constantly stirring, until the custard reaches 184° F on a thermometer. Stir in the gelatin and cook until the gelatin is completely dissolved. Remove the pan from

the heat and set in a bowl of ice. Stir occasionally and allow the custard to cool.

Whip the cream until soft peaks form. Once the custard is completely cooled, slowly fold in the cream.

To MAKE THE RASPBERRY MOUSSE, sprinkle the gelatin over the water in a small bowl to soften. Puree one cup of fresh or frozen berries that have been thawed, with a tablespoon of sugar. Strain and discard the seeds.

Bring the raspberry puree to a gentle boil in a small saucepan. Combine the egg yolks and sugar in a small bowl and whisk until well combined. Pour a small amount of the hot raspberries into the yolk mixture and stir well to temper the eggs. Immediately stir the egg yolk mixture into the saucepan and cook, constantly stirring, until the custard reaches 184° F on a thermometer. Stir in the gelatin and cook until the gelatin is completely dissolved. Remove the pan from the heat and set in a bowl of ice water. Stir occasionally and allow the custard to cool.

Whip the cream until soft peaks form. Once the custard is completely cooled, slowly fold in the cream.

To MAKE THE COCOA SAUCE, combine the cocoa, sugar, and salt in a small saucepan. Slowly stir in the water. Bring to a boil, decrease the heat, and simmer for a few minutes until it has thickened. Strain into a container and refrigerate.

To ASSEMBLE THE CAKE, set out a half sheet pan and line with parchment paper. Set out a rectangular metal frame measuring 10 1/2-inches by 15 1/2-inches inside this sheet pan. Trim both layers of the chocolate sponge to fit snuggly inside the frame.

Fit one cake layer inside the frame. Spread the Key lime mousse evenly on top of the chocolate sponge.

Give it a light rap on the table to remove excess air bubbles. Gently place the second trimmed layer of sponge on top of this. Spread the raspberry mousse on top of the second sponge. Again gently rap this on the counter to remove air bubbles. Place the cake in the freezer for 24 hours.

To FINISH ASSEMBLING THE DESSERT, line a clean half sheet pan with parchment paper. Run a warm knife around the edge of the frame and remove. Cut the cake into 4-inch by 1 1/2-inch bars. Transfer these bars to a clean pan or platter so that you may arrange berries on the top surface. Garnish with fresh raspberries so that the entire top of the cake is covered.

To SERVE, lay one bar that is already garnished diagonally across a plate. Place a drop of the cocoa sauce about the size of a quarter at the end closest to you and draw it away from you with the back of the spoon. Garnish the plate with a chocolate curl.

PIES & TARTS

No other dessert harkens back to childhood, holidays, and all the sweet memories of momma's kitchen, as does a pie. It can be served simple and unadorned, or piled high with fruit and cream—we love them!

All save one of the dishes in this chapter are refinements of classic recipes, using local ingredients—muscadine grapes, peaches, and that old Southern staple, buttermilk. The exception is Anson's Pecan Pie Reconstruction (I'm assuming that the title is a gentle pun on the war that many Southerners politely refer to as "that recent unpleasantness"). The separate tastes of this deconstruction equal the essence of the original classic.

Lovely waterfront mansions along East Battery Street are part of the famed Battery Row, and date from as early as 1810. On these rooftops, Charlestonians stood and watched shots fired on Fort Sumter that began the Civil War. The remains of a Confederate cannon that exploded are still embedded in a dormer room at Number 9 East Battery.

ANSON RESTAURANT

PECAN PIE RECONSTRUCTION

This dessert was developed by Pastry Chef Julie R. Thigpen for Anson Chef Kevin Johnson to use in a cooking class. The tastes are a modern spin on the traditional Southern pecan pie. It was a huge hit at their class, so the chefs decided to make it part of their regular menu.

SERVES 8

CHOCOLATE BOURBON MOUSSE

8 ounces good-quality eating chocolate
   (dark, milk, semisweet, etc.)
2 cups heavy cream
1 large egg yolk
1 large whole egg
2 tablespoons bourbon

For PRALINE recipe, see page 91

BOURBON GELÉE

2 tablespoons plus 1/2 cup water
1 (1/4-ounce) packet unflavored gelatin
1/2 cup granulated white sugar
1/2 cup bourbon

VANILLA MILK SHAKE

1 cup vanilla ice cream
1 cup half-and-half

TO MAKE THE MOUSSE, melt the chocolate in a metal bowl set over a saucepan of simmering water, stirring occasionally with a rubber spatula, until melted and smooth.

Meanwhile, whip the cream in an electric mixer fitted with a wire whisk attachment until soft peaks form.

Combine the egg and the egg yolk in a clean mixing bowl and whisk on high speed until very fluffy and pale yellow in color. Mix in the bourbon. Quickly but gently fold the egg mixture into the chocolate. Then in three batches, fold the whipped cream into the chocolate mixture.

Fill eight 4-ounce ramekins evenly with the mousse, leaving 1/8 of an inch of space at the top of each ramekin. Smooth the top of the mousse flat with the back of a spoon. Place in the refrigerator for at least 1 hour to set.

TO MAKE THE BOURBON GELÉE, pour 2 tablespoons water into a small bowl, and sprinkle the gelatin over it. Let stand a few minutes to soften. Combine the remaining 1/2 cup water and the white sugar in a small saucepan and bring just to a boil. Remove from the heat and add the gelatin mixture, stirring them together until all the gelatin is dissolved. Stir in the bourbon last. Allow the mixture to cool to about 90° F.

Pour a very thin layer over each mousse-filled ramekin. Return to the refrigerator for 3 to 4 hours to completely set.

JUST BEFORE SERVING, MAKE THE MILK SHAKE. Combine the ice cream and half-and-half in a blender and blend on high speed until smooth and creamy.

TO ASSEMBLE THE DESSERT, place each ramekin of the mousse on a large plate and place several pralines to one side, next to the mousse. Fill eight 2-ounce shot glasses with the vanilla shake and place on the plates opposite the mousse. Serve immediately.

This is a local favorite, with many windows for taking in the scenes of the Historic District, such as the passing horse-drawn carriages. Situated in the Old City Market, it's reminiscent of an antebellum ballroom, with its golden chairs, beveled-glass plantation doors and antique oil paintings. The ironwork on its façade may conjure the French Quarter, but the interior is decidedly Low Country elegance.

Anson serves up classic Southern fare, but strives to make it extraordinary. The Shrimp and Grits, a favorite dish, is made with white corn, ground to a sand-fine texture with a stone grinder, and topped with plump Carolina shrimp.

Anson is a sunny, busy, high-visibility dining experience that becomes softly lit and romantic at night. Charleston locals are assured of running into familiar faces and catching up on the latest news and gossip, and even tourists may leave having made new acquaintances. Southern hospitality and refined cuisine keep folks coming back.

CIRCA 1886
LEMON BUTTERMILK TART

SERVES 6 TO 8

TART SHELL

1 1/4 cups all-purpose flour
1 tablespoon sugar
1/2 teaspoon salt
1/2 cup chilled unsalted butter, cut into pieces
1/4 cup ice water
1/4 teaspoon white vinegar

BUTTERMILK FILLING

3 large eggs
1 3/4 cups sugar
1 cup whole buttermilk
1 1/2 teaspoons vanilla extract
Zest of 1 lemon, finely grated
1 1/2 teaspoons all-purpose flour
1/2 teaspoon baking powder
1/2 cup unsalted butter, melted

To make the tart shell, combine the flour, sugar, and salt in an electric mixer with a paddle attachment. Add the cold butter and mix until the butter is pea-sized. Add the water and the vinegar. Mix until just incorporated. Remove the dough from the bowl, form into a disk, and wrap in plastic wrap. Chill for at least 1 hour.

Roll out the dough on a lightly floured surface to a circle of about 10 inches. Fit the dough into a 9-inch tart pan, folding in and crimping the edges of the dough to make the walls of the tart shell strong.

Chill for 15 minutes. Meanwhile preheat the oven to 350° F.

Line the pastry shell with a piece of aluminum foil and fill with dried beans or pie weights. Bake for 8 to 10 minutes, until the dough is a light golden brown.

Remove from the oven and let cool on a wire rack. Decrease the oven temperature to 300° F.

To make the filling, combine the eggs, sugar, buttermilk, vanilla, and lemon zest. Whisk by hand until well combined. Whisk in the flour and baking powder. Finally whisk in the melted butter. Pour into the partially baked tart shell.

Bake for 45 minutes, until the filling is golden and mostly set (it will still be wobbly in the center.) Let cool on a wire rack. Serve warm or cold.

Set in the red-brick carriage house of the Wentworth Mansion, Circa 1886 has the ambiance of a cloistered estate. A little off the beaten path, in a quiet residential area of the Historic District, this 5-star restaurant has won national recognition, Wine Spectator's Award of Excellence, and the prestigious DiRoNA Award.

Circa 1886 was opened in 2000, and is part of the Charming Inns family of historical bed and breakfasts. Within the manicured grounds of the Empire-style Wentworth Mansion you'll find a path leading to the restaurant lined with crepe myrtles. The carriage house restaurant kept its original stable doors, a kitchen fireplace, and is warmly lit to create a timeless, elegant atmosphere.

Charleston native Emily Cookson, pastry chef of Circa 1886, comes from a long line of self-taught candy makers. She carries on a tradition that goes back to her great-grandmother, who roasted nuts and used them in candy creations to sell during the Depression. She uses her great-uncle's marble candy slab now, one that he used to make "humbug candy", a hard peppermint. Cookson finds inspiration from those Southern sweet-making roots to create fabulous desserts for Circa 1886.

LA FOURCHETTE
TARTE TARTIN

Chef Goulet says that Tarte Tartin was created by the Tartin sisters, who popularized it in their restaurant at Lamotte-Beuvron, south of Orléans, in the Loire Valley, in the early 20th century.

SERVES 6 TO 8

La Fourchette is a French bistro on upper King Street that's a hit with the locals for its comfort food in an informal setting. Their pommes frites are gaining fame, owing their particular flavor to being twice-fried in duck fat.

The Charleston Post and Courier *gave La Fourchette the "Fabulous French" distinction in its annual review of restaurants. Francophiles, including local Charleston chefs, are particularly drawn to its cozy Parisian ambiance. Gallic-inspired music, red walls and bistro posters all lend a romantic European feel to the place.*

There's little pretense, but a lot of hearty French favorites, including homemade pate. Kevin Kelley, owner of Vintage, consults on the wine list for La Fourchette, and makes suggestions that pair wines with the hearty peasant fare.

PASTRY

1 cup all-purpose flour
1 tablespoon sugar
1/2 teaspoon salt
6 tablespoons chilled unsalted butter, cut into small pieces

FILLING

1 1/2 cups sugar
1 1/4 cups unsalted butter, cut into small pieces
9 Golden Delicious or Roma apples, peeled, cored and halved

Vanilla ice cream, to serve

TO PREPARE THE PASTRY, combine the flour, sugar, and salt in a deep mixing bowl. Add the butter and cut in with a pastry cutter or two knives until the mixture resembles coarse crumbs. Form into a ball, wrap in plastic wrap, and let rest for 1 hour.

Preheat the oven to 400° F.

TO PREPARE THE APPLES, combine the sugar and butter in a 10-inch oven-safe sauté pan over medium heat and cook until the sugar has caramelized and is light blond in color. Arrange the apple slices (skinned side down) in the caramel. Decrease the heat and cook until apples become soft, about 5 minutes.

On a lightly floured surface, roll out the pastry to a thickness of 1/4 inch. Place on top of the apples in the sauté pan. Being careful not to burn your fingers, gently tuck the edges of dough against the inside of the pan.

Bake for 25 to 30 minutes, until the pastry is golden brown

Let cool on a wire rack for about 20 minutes. Loosen the sides of the tart by running a knife all around the inside edge. Place a large serving plate on top of the pan and invert.

Serve with warm with vanilla ice cream.

IRVIN HOUSE
ANN LIMEHOUSE IRVIN'S MUSCADINE GRAPE HULL PIE

This is a traditional recipe that Ann says reminds her of growing up in the country and sitting on the front porch, enjoying family and food. She was creative and used a tart pan for this, and fashioned grape leaf shapes out of the crust for the top. It makes a pretty difference!

SERVES 6 TO 8

1 heaping quart of ripe muscadine grapes
1 1/4 cups sugar, plus additional sugar for sprinkling
1 1/2 tablespoons fresh lemon juice
2 tablespoons all-purpose flour
1/4 teaspoon salt
1/4 teaspoon ground cinnamon

9-inch pie shell with lattice strips, homemade or store-bought
Egg white, lightly beaten

Squeeze the pulp from the hulls of the grapes. Boil the hulls in a small amount of water for 30 minutes. Stir in 1/4 cup of the sugar until dissolved. Set aside

Add the remaining 1 cup sugar to the grape pulp and juice. Bring to a boil and boil gently for about 20 minutes. Let cool.

Press the pulp through a colander to remove the seeds, mashing it down with a spoon. Drain the hulls and add to the pulp mixture. Discard the seeds and put hulls into the liquid.

Preheat the oven to 400° F.

Form a smooth paste by mixing together the lemon juice, flour, salt, and cinnamon. Stir into the pulp and hull mixture. Pour into a pie shell and add lattice strips on top, or decorate according to your taste. Brush with egg whites and sprinkle sugar on top.

Bake for 10 minutes. Decrease the oven temperature to 350° F and continue baking for 20 minutes. Let cool before serving.

Establishing the Irvin House Vineyards in 2001 brought Jim and Ann Irvin full circle in their lives, having both grown up on family farms. They've created Charleston's only domestic winery on their 48-acre Wadmalaw Island property, one that has five labels, and is a regional attraction for visitors. It's a place that feels like another country and another time, and is well-worth the drive from the city.

By making muscadine-based wines, the Irvins bring back a taste familiar to many Southerners. Muscadine was once called the fountain of youth, for its high levels of resveratrol, an antioxidant that lowers cholesterol and reduces the risk for heart disease.

The five wines were given names inspired by the vineyard setting —Palmetto, Tara Gold, Magnolia, Mullet Hall Red, and Live Oak Reserve. The Irvins convey their love of the vineyard and the process of winemaking by their enthusiasm and friendliness.

For the visitor, there are tours, tastings, a gift shop and at harvest time, the Family Harvest Stomp, where everyone can try their hand at grape crushing in bare feet. And, if you're lucky, Ann will have made one of her tasty pies.

BANANA PUDDING PIE REDO

This recipe has been so popular at the bakery that many of Chris's catering customers bring their own plates for her to use to bake the pie.

SERVES 8

FILLING

2 cups whole milk
1 teaspoon vanilla extract
4 large egg yolks
1/3 cup superfine sugar
1/4 cup superfine sugar, for the whipped
  cream on top
1/3 cup cornstarch
2 cups heavy cream
3 bananas, sliced
20 whole vanilla wafers to assemble, 3 to
  stand on the top to finish it

CRUST

2 cups ground vanilla wafers
1/2 cup granulated white sugar
1/2 cup unsalted butter, melted

Preheat the oven to 350° F.

To make the crust, combine the ground vanilla wafers, white sugar, and melted butter in a bowl and mix well. Press evenly into a 9-inch deep pie dish, or regular 10-inch pie dish, to form a crust. Bake for 10 to 15 minutes, until lightly browned.

Cool on a wire rack.

To make the filling, combine the milk and vanilla in a heavy saucepan over medium-high heat and bring to a boil.

Whisk the egg yolk and 1/3 cup of the superfine sugar in a bowl until thick and pale. Whisk in the cornstarch. Slowly pour in the hot milk, whisking continuously. Pour the mixture back into the saucepan and cook over medium heat, whisking until thick. Remove from heat, transfer to a glass bowl, cover with plastic wrap directly on the pastry cream, set aside to cool.

Combine the cream and remaining 1/4 cup superfine sugar in an electric mixer fitted with a whip attachment. Whip until firm. Fold 1 cup of the whipped cream into the cool pastry cream.

To assemble the pie, spoon the pastry cream into the crust, alternating with the sliced bananas and whole vanilla wafers. Spread the remaining whipped cream on top. Chill before serving.

COBBLERS, COMPOTES & TRIFLES

Each year for the past ten, Charleston has been named the "Best-Mannered City in America" by etiquette expert Marjabelle Young Stewart, who has compiled the list for 28 years. It is refreshing to know that charm, manners, hospitality and friendliness still exist to such a high degree in this Southern city.

Food is always sweeter when served with a smile, and those are the good-natured manners you'll invariably experience in most Charleston restaurants. These delicious desserts won't need much to sweeten their taste, though. Based on available seasonal fruits, these delicious cobblers, compotes, and trifles will have you calling for seconds and thirds. Just be sure to remember your manners!

Voted one of the Best New Restaurants in America in 2006 by Esquire Magazine, *Cordavi serves up eclectic nouvelle cuisine in a sleek, hip setting. The name sounds Italian, but is actually an amalgam of the two young chefs first names.*

Corey Elliott and David Szlam partnered to open Cordavi and add a decidedly non-traditional restaurant to Charleston's fine dining scene. The menu as a global flair, but draws on local ingredients, as well. The complex selections can be sampled in multiple course pairings, and courses are transitioned with amuse bouches.

There's a cool bar setting with jazz on Wednesday nights. Rich red walls lend a vibrancy, while white tablecloths on the tables with a single fresh flower add simple elegance. Elliot and Szlam are aiming for a synchronized culinary experience that meets the expectations of the most discriminating fine dining clientele.

CORDAVI RESTAURANT
ROASTED PLUM COBBLER

Pastry Chef Susanna Ieronemo swears this is her favorite "comfort" dessert, warm and satisfying. she serves it with a Cinnamon-Rosemary ice cream that is just perfect.

SERVES 6 TO 8

ROASTED PLUMS

1 1/2 cups water
1/2 cup rosé or other light wine
1/2 cup granulated white sugar
1/4 cup firmly packed brown sugar
1/4 cup honey
Pinch of salt
1/2 vanilla bean
Cinnamon stick
Freshly grated nutmeg
2 to 3 slices fresh ginger
6 to 8 plums

For CINNAMON-ROSEMARY ICE CREAM, see page 90

CANDIED ALMOND PASTRY

1 1/2 cups all-purpose flour
1 cup almond flour
1/2 cup granulated sugar, plus more for dusting
1 teaspoon salt
1 cup unsalted butter, cut into 1/2-inch pieces and frozen
1/4 teaspoon vanilla extract
1/4 cup ice water
1 egg, lightly beaten with 1 tablespoon of water for an egg wash

Sprigs of rosemary
Sliced almonds

Preheat the oven to 400° F.

To PREPARE THE PLUMS, combine the water, wine, white sugar, brown sugar, honey, salt, vanilla bean, cinnamon stick, nutmeg, and ginger in a saucepan. Bring to a simmer and simmer for 10 minutes. Remove from the heat and let steep for another 5 minutes. Remove the spices and reserve the liquid.

Slice the plums into halves and remove the pits. Place cut side down in a roasting pan with 1 1/2-inch to 2-inch sides. Pour in enough liquid to come up 1/4 inch in the pan. Reserve any extra liquid.

Roast for about 10 minutes, until the plums are easily pierced with a fork.

Immediately remove the plums and reserve the liquid to add to the cut plums. Cool the plums in refrigerator. When cool, remove the skins and cut into large chunks.

To MAKE THE PASTRY, mix together the white and almond flours, 1/2 cup sugar, and salt in an electric mixer fitted with a paddle attachment. Add the butter and mix at low speed, until butter in the mixture resembles crumbs. Add the vanilla to the water and slowly add to bowl. Mix until a dough is formed. Roll out the dough between two pieces of parchment paper to a thickness of 1/4 inch. Transfer to a baking sheet, still on the parchment paper, and freeze for 10 minutes.

Preheat the oven to 400° F. Cut the pastry into a desired shape, or with a 3-inch round cookie cutter. Brush with the egg wash and sprinkle with sugar.

Bake for about 10 minutes, until the sugar is bubbly and the edges are golden. Remove from pan quickly, before the sugar hardens, and cool on wire racks.

To ASSEMBLE THE DESSERT, heat the plums in the reserved liquid. Divide the plums among six to eight individual serving bowls. Top with a piece of the candied almond pastry and a scoop of cinnamon-rosemary ice cream. Garnish with a few sprigs of rosemary and sliced almonds and serve.

SIX TABLES

Chef Jeremy Holst's Blackberry Cobbler

Chef Holst says that this is his version of his grandmother's cobbler, served warm for Sunday dinners. The fillings can be changed with the season, and the dish enjoyed year-round.

SERVES 6

TOPPING

2 cups all-purpose flour
1 1/2 teaspoons sugar
1/2 teaspoon salt
1 cup solid vegetable shortening
1/2 cup ice water

Vanilla ice cream or whipped cream, to serve
Mint leaves, to garnish.

FILLING

6 cups fresh blackberries
2 cups sugar
1 tablespoon ground cinnamon
1 tablespoon water

2 tablespoon all-purpose flour

The experience at Six Tables has been likened to an intimate European dinner party where the host has gone missing. The evening begins with a glass of champagne and a warm welcome from the chef.

The decor is baroque and rococo, with fine linens draped over just a few tables in the small dining room. There's only one seating per night, with a prix fix meal that includes six courses of classic French and New American cuisine.

Six Tables is a chain restaurant, with 8 locations, most of them in southern Florida. But by offering highly personal service and the pageantry of ritualized fine dining, many diners consider it a culinary adventure.

To MAKE THE TOPPING, sift the flour, sugar, and salt into a large mixing bowl. Cut in the shortening with a pastry cutter or two knives until the mixture resembles coarse crumbs. Add the water, 1 tablespoon at a time, and work the dough until you have a smooth ball. Wrap the dough tightly with plastic wrap and refrigerate for 45 minutes.

Preheat the oven to 350° F. Grease an 8-inch baking dish.

Remove the dough from refrigerator. Place on a lightly floured surface and roll out the dough with a rolling pin until it is 1/8 inch thick. Cut out circles with a 2-inch round cutter.

To PREPARE THE FILLING, combine the blackberries, sugar, cinnamon, and water in a medium saucepan over medium-low heat. Lightly sprinkle 2 tablespoons flour over the berries as they cook to thicken. Cook for 5 minutes, or until berries begin to soften. Pour the berries into the prepared baking dish. Top with the dough circles.

Bake for 25 to 30 minutes, until the dough is golden brown.

To SERVE, spoon onto dessert plates. Top with ice cream or whipped cream and garnish with mint.

The acronym is SNOB, but with its club feel and open kitchen, it's fine dining without the pretension. Chef Frank Lee is a native Carolinian that is a warm presence in the kitchen, smiling under his chili pepper patterned baseball cap. Diners can watch the culinary alchemy unfold, making the entire experience more interactive.

Slightly North of Broad's cuisine centers on the Low Country's multicultural heritage. Chef Lee grew up on Gullah flavors during summers at Sullivan's Island, and still draws inspiration from the African roots of many traditional Southern dishes.

SNOB is a consistent local favorite, as well as being featured nationally on shows like ABC's Good Morning America and the Today Show. It's housed in a 19th century brick warehouse, which gives it the feel of old Charleston.

The SNOB dining experience is like being in a comfortable home with a lot of friends. The lighting is just right, and the ambience is lively, chatty, and fun.

SLIGHTLY NORTH OF BROAD
CHEF FRANK LEE'S PEACH COBBLER

This traditional Southern dessert is served in a great many Charleston restaurants, but nowhere better than here. The bourbon is the secret ingredient.

SERVES 4 TO 5

FILLING

8 cups peeled and sliced peaches
1/2 cup bourbon (or to taste)
1/2 cup sugar
1/2 teaspoon vanilla extract

TOPPING

1/2 cup unsalted butter, at room temperature
1 cup sugar
1 large egg
1/2 cup sour cream
1 cup all-purpose flour
1 teaspoon baking powder
1 teaspoon ground cinnamon

TO MAKE THE FILLING, combine the peaches, bourbon, sugar, and vanilla in a bowl. Let stand for at least 30 minutes to macerate. (It can be left overnight in the refrigerator.)

Preheat the oven to 325° F.

TO MAKE THE TOPPING, cream the butter and sugar together until light and fluffy. Mix in the egg. Fold in the sour cream.

Sift together the flour, baking powder, and cinnamon into a separate bowl. Fold into the butter mixture.

TO ASSEMBLE THE COBBLER, spoon 2 cups of the peach filling into each individual 3-cup ungreased baking dish. Top with about 1 cup of the topping mixture, dolloping it onto the cobbler mixture.

Bake for 40 to 50 minutes, until the topping is golden and the juices are bubbling. Serve warm or hot, with ice cream.

MITCHELL CROSBY
CHARLESTON TRIFLE

Crosby says, "The lovely thing about trifle is that it is truly a formula, but it is open to the interpretation of the maker and the products available. We get bored with specialty jams about halfway through the jar. Hence, a great reason at the end of the year to make a trifle and use up what is left over."

SERVES 12

CAKE LAYERS
2 homemade loaves of a butter pound cake

SWEETENED WHIPPED CREAM
1 pint whipping cream
Sugar
Vanilla extract

SPIRIT LAYERS
1/2 to 3/4 cup total, equal parts white rum
   and cream Sherry (American Sherry is fine)

Whipped cream

FRUIT SPREAD LAYERS
1 cup jams or jellies (seedless recommended),
   to complement your fruits, at room temperature

FRUITS
2 large peaches, skins on, pitted, and
   sliced into eighths
1 pint raspberries
1 pint blackberries
1 pint blueberries
1/2 (8.8-ounce) bottle Toschi Amarena wild
   cherries in syrup (optional)

Sprigs of mint

TO PREPARE THE CAKE LAYERS, break a third of the cake by hand into crumbs. Tear the remaining cake into small bites.

TO PREPARE THE WHIPPED CREAM LAYER, beat the cream with sugar and vanilla to taste until soft peaks form.

TO ASSEMBLE THE TRIFLE, set aside your best-looking fruit for the top. In a clear glass trifle bowl, begin with a layer of cake, a sprinkle of the spirits to moisten, a layer of jam spread with a spatula, whipped cream, and then fruit. Repeat. Remember that you want this to look colorful and interesting from the outside. Hence, be mindful to spread all layers to the outer edges as you go. We usually reserve the peaches for the center of the trifle edges and then for the top. Because they are larger and of a different color palette, they show up very well!

If you really want the magic touch, Crosby advises adding a half jar of Toschi brand Amarena cherries onto the center of your top. These are wild Italian cherries soaked in a thick cherry sauce made without alcohol and processed with a secret 80-year-old technique. Truly the secret ingredient that no one will be able to figure out!

You can make this up to 8 hours in advance. Holding the trifle longer than that causes the cake to get soggy and the rum and sherry can become overbearing.

Serve this with an extra bowl of whipped cream at the table, should anyone desire it for a bit of topping, as well as fresh sprigs of mint to garnish. This is an excellent item to serve from your sideboard while guests are dining at the table, or on a counter where your guests can enjoy seeing this marvel, and watching you serve it.

With roots going back to 1670 in Colleton County, Mitchell Crosby intimately knows the region, its people and traditions. He is sought out as an event planner and caterer because of this combination of knowledge, creativity, and experience.

For many years, Crosby was the meeting manager at Charleston Place, putting on successful events for high-end clients like BMW of North America and the Family Circle Cup. In 2004, he started his own company, JMC Charleston, with a team assembled to plan destination travel and themed events in grand Low Country style.

He currently operates two venues for events, Crosby's Docks and the Calhoun Mansion. Crosby is the entertainment/style editor for Charleston *and* Charleston Home *magazines, and he's also been featured in* Town & Country *magazine, and* Every Day with Rachel Ray.

SOUTHERN FRIED PEACHES WITH BOURBON BLUEBERRY COMPOTE

SERVES 4

POUND CAKE

10-inch cake pan
2 1/2 cups all-purpose flour
1 teaspoons baking powder
Pinch of salt
1/2 cup butter, at room temperature
1 cups granulated white sugar
2/3 cups firmly packed brown sugar
1/2 teaspoon vanilla extract
2 large eggs, at room temperature
2/3 cups milk, at room temperature

Vanilla bean ice cream, to serve

BOURBON BLUEBERRY COMPOTE

1 pint blueberries
1 teaspoon ground cinnamon
Zest and juice of 1 lemon
Pinch of salt
1/2 cup granulated white sugar
Bourbon

FRIED PEACHES

4 Large Ripe Peaches
1 large egg
Pinch of salt
Pinch of ground cinnamon
1 cup all-purpose flour
Oil, for frying

A gastropub is the London equivalent of a Paris brasserie, a place where you can expect fine cuisine in a pub setting. The Red Drum Gastropub in Mt. Pleasant is the creation of husband-wife team Marianna and Ben Berryhill. It's been mentioned in the New York Times as one of the best restaurants in Charleston.

There's a Southwestern influence in cuisine and décor. The Berryhills come to Charleston by way of Houston, where they ran the front and back of the well-known Café Annie. Chef Berryhill also had a weekly food show that won him regional celebrity.

Red Drum offers a comfortable dining experience, with an outdoor patio with woodburning fireplace, and a wine room with an impressive floor-to-ceiling display of the restaurant's collection of labels.

Preheat the oven to 350° F. Coat a 10-inch cake pan with nonstick spray and set aside.

To make the cake, combine the flour, baking powder, and salt in a medium mixing bowl. Set aside. Combine the butter, white sugar, and brown sugar in an electric mixer fitted with a paddle attachment. Beat at medium speed until light and creamy. Add the vanilla and eggs, one at a time, beating after each addition until the egg is fully incorporated, remembering to scrape down the sides of the bowl frequently. Alternately add the milk and flour mixture in three batches, mixing low speed until well blended. Pour into the prepared pan.

Bake for 20 minutes, until golden brown and a tester inserted near the center comes out clean.

Cool completely on a wire rack. Once cooled, remove from the pan and break into chunks. Spread out the pieces in the pan and return to the oven to dry for about 10 minutes. Once the chunks have cooled down place in food processor and grind until fine crumbs. It is best to do this when completely cool so the cake does not clump.

To prepare the blueberry compote, combine the blueberries, cinnamon, lemon zest and juice, salt, and white sugar in a medium saucepan over medium heat. Cook, stirring occasionally, until the blueberries release their juice, about 10 minutes. Remove from the heat, transfer to a bowl, and stir in bourbon to taste. Keep warm.

To prepare the peaches, be sure to choose ones that are fully ripe. To peel the peaches, dip each

one in a pot of boiling water for about 30 seconds to loose the skins. Then peel each peach, cut in half, and remove the pit. With a melon baller, remove a circle of peach flesh where the pit previously sat, creating a nice hole for the sauce.

Begin heating a deep fryer or tall, narrow saucepan with oil to 350° F.

To coat the peaches, beat the egg with the salt and cinnamon in a shallow bowl. Put the flour and the pound cake crumbs in separate shallow bowls.

When the oil is hot, dip each peach half in the egg wash, then in the flour, in the egg wash again, and then in the cake crumbs, turning to coat each peach completely.

Gently slip a few peaches at a time into the hot oil, taking care not to crowd the pan. Fry until the crumbs are golden brown, this should take about 2-3 minutes. Remove from the oil with tongs, and place on paper towels to drain. Repeat until all the peaches are coated and fried. (The peaches can be made in advance but crisp again in a 350 degree oven for 5-7 minutes before serving.)

TO SERVE, place a peach half on each dessert place. Spoon the compote into the hole where the pit had been. Top with the ice cream, and serve immediately.

CUSTARDS
& PUDDINGS

Sweetgrass basketmaking in the Charleston area can be traced back to the slaves who were brought over from West Africa 300 years ago. The art form has been passed down through generations, and these beautiful functional baskets still grace local tables, and are sold at the open-air downtown market and at roadside stands.

The "sweetgrass" used to weave these traditional baskets has the sweet smell of fresh hay, which gave it the name. Water will not hurt the sweetgrass, so the baskets can be washed and rinsed, which makes them very durable.

Traditions are important to keep alive, and the English influence that brought custards and puddings to the South has inspired some wonderful desserts. The Carolina Gold Rice used for Fig Chef Mike Lata's Rice Pudding is a perfect example of a traditional dish. Magnolia's Sweet Biscuits with Orange Custard Sauce is another that you will enjoy.

FIG CAFE
CAROLINA GOLD RICE PUDDING

SERVES 8

2 tablespoons confectioners' sugar	1 cinnamon stick
1 cup Carolina Gold Rice	3 large egg yolks
7 cups whole milk	16 fresh figs, to serve
1 vanilla bean (or extract to taste)	Granulated white sugar
1 cup sugar	Chopped pistachios, roasted, to garnish

With the mantra that "food is good", Chef Mike Lata wins raves for keeping things simple, and letting the natural flavor of locally grown foods come through. The menu changes seasonally, and sometimes daily, with great care to pick ingredients at their peak. Chef Lata is a founding member of Slow Food Charleston and has been a champion of locally grown produce.

Chef Lata and owner-manager Adam Nemirow, both formerly of Anson, opened Fig in 2001 as a neighborhood bistro. Familiar with the Charleston restaurant scene, they wanted to create a relaxed place for fine dining. Long banquettes and community tables encourage neighborly togetherness.

The décor is paired down to a minimalist look, primarily painted in earth tones with splashes of color here and there. The retro-classic elements make it hip in design, but without the pretension. Fig focuses on creative cuisine that's kept simple, in an environment with just the meaningful essentials.

Fig has been included in Gourmet magazine's list of Where to Eat Now in 30 American Cities. Mike Lata was a finalist for the James Beard Foundation Award for Best Chef in the Southeast for 2007.

Bring 4 cups water to a boil with the confectioners' sugar. Add the rice and blanch for about 5 minutes. Drain the rice and rinse.

Combine the blanched rice with the milk, vanilla, sugar, and cinnamon stick in a heavy saucepan. Bring to a simmer. Cook until rice is very tender. Remove from the heat. Remove the cinnamon stick. Whisk the egg yolks into the milk and rice mixture. (The heat of the mixture will cook the egg yolks.)

Pour into a casserole dish, cover, and refrigerate for at least 3 hours before serving. The pudding can also be served at room temperature.

To serve, cut the figs in half, sprinkle with white sugar, and run them under a blow torch to caramelize the sugar, or serve the cut figs plain. Garnish the figs with a sprinkling of pistachios.

Croissant Bread Pudding with Roasted Pecans, Bourbon Drunken Raisins, and Warm Coconut Caramel

Bread pudding is a typical American recipe, and Master Pastry Chef Vinzenz Aschbacher has tweaked this by substituting stale croissants for the usual bread. It's a wonderfully rich pudding!

SERVES 6

The Palmetto Café is an informal restaurant open for breakfast and lunch, set inside the opulent Charleston Place Hotel. Just off the hotel's grand lobby of Italian marble, guests can relax from the business of shopping or sightseeing in this garden setting.

There's a lush courtyard with a circular bronze fountain, and the airy space is often sun-dappled. It's an unhurried atmosphere, where diners can linger over coffee and desserts, or come for the weekend brunch.

Charleston Place is an 18th-century building with many 5-star amenities, including a European-style spa. It's been named one of the Top 10 Hotels in North America by Conde Nast Traveler *magazine and awarded the AAA 4-Diamond rating.*

BREAD PUDDING

1 1/4 cups raisins
2 cups Jim Beam bourbon
5 large eggs
5 large egg yolks
1 cup firmly packed brown sugar
1/2 cup granulated white sugar
2 cups heavy cream

2 teaspoons ground cinnamon
1 vanilla bean, scraped
1 cup pecans
1 teaspoon caramel extract
8 large day-old croissants

For COCONUT CARAMEL SAUCE recipe, see page 93

TO MAKE THE BREAD PUDDING, combine the raisins and Jim Beam in a small bowl and let plump for 15 to 30 minutes.

Preheat the oven to 350° F.

Meanwhile, in a large bowl, whisk together the whole eggs, egg yolks, and brown and white sugars and set aside.

In a small saucepan, heat the cream, cinnamon, and vanilla. Bring to a boil. Slowly pour a little of the hot cream mixture into the egg mixture. Continue to whisk in small amounts of milk at a time until the temperature of the two mixtures are equal. Whisk all of the egg mixture into the cream mixture. Whisk in the raisins, pecans, and caramel along with the remaining soaking liquid.

Slice the croissants into 2-inch cubes and stir into the egg mixture. Let soak for 15 minutes. Spoon into 8-ounce ovenproof bowls or ramekins

Bake for 45 minutes, or until golden.

TO SERVE, warm the sauce in the top of a double boiler. Spoon the sauce over the bowls of warm bread pudding and serve.

OLD VILLAGE POST HOUSE
CHOCOLATE POTS DE CRÈME

SERVES 6

2 cups whipping cream	6 large egg yolks
1/2 cup whole milk	1/3 cup sugar
5 ounces bittersweet or semisweet chocolate, chopped	White chocolate, to garnish
	6 strawberries, to garnish

Preheat the oven to 325° F.

Combine the cream and milk in heavy saucepan over medium heat. Bring to a simmer. Remove from the heat. Add the chocolate; whisk until melted and smooth.

Whisk the yolks and sugar in large bowl to blend. Gradually whisk in the hot chocolate mixture. Strain the mixture into another bowl. Cool for 10 minutes, skimming any foam from the surface.

Divide the custard mixture among six 3/4-cup custard cups or soufflé dishes. Cover each with aluminum foil. Place the cups in a large baking pan. Add enough hot water to the pan to come halfway up the sides of the cups.

Bake for about 55 minutes, until the custards are set but the centers are still wobbly.

Remove the cups from the water. Remove the foil. Chill the custards until cold, about 3 hours.

TO SERVE, shave white chocolate over each the custard. Top each with a strawberry.

Opened in 2003, this quaint inn is part of the Maverick Southern Kitchens Group, along with High Cotton and Slightly North of Broad. The Old Village Post House is in a restored 19th-century building within the historic and picturesque fishing community of Mt. Pleasant.

It's meant to remind travelers of the wayside inns of days gone by, where neighbors would gather for an unhurried evening. The tavern has a classic look with warm wood and large leather chairs. The dining room is elegant and airy, in the style of a Southern bistro.

Chef Tim Armstrong seeks out fresh, light ways of preparing traditional Southern favorites. Maverick's sommelier Patrick Emmerson assists with the wine pairings, with special event dinners featuring wines of a particular region. The brunch beverages include the Mimosa, but go beyond with the Pimms #1 Cup, the classic English punch and an intriguing drink called the Post House Painkiller.

MUSE RESTAURANT
Limoncello Parfait

This graceful and tangy little dessert has won awards and been featured in local magazines.

SERVES 6

4 large egg yolks
1/2 cup sugar
1/4 cup limoncello
1 cup whipping cream
Fresh raspberries, to garnish

RASPBERRY COULIS

1 pint raspberries
3 tablespoons sugar
2 teaspoons lemon juice

PHYLO DISC

4 sheets phylo dough
1/4 cup clarified butter
4 tablespoons sugar

Fresh raspberries to garnish

Combine the egg yolks, 1/4 cup of the sugar, and the limoncello in a metal bowl. The bowl should be set over simmering water to cook the egg yolks as the mixture is beaten. Beat until the mixture forms a thick ribbon when the beaters are lifted. Set the bowl in a larger bowl of ice and continue to beat until cold.

Whip the cream with the remaining 1/4 cup sugar until it forms stiff peaks. Fold the whipped cream into the limoncello mixture. Freeze for 3 hours.

To make the raspberry coulis, puree the raspberries, lemon juice, and sugar in a blender. Push the puree through a fine mesh strainer until there is nothing left in the strainer except seeds.

To make the phylo disc, paint one sheet of phylo dough with clarified butter using a pastry brush. Sprinkle 1 tablespoon of sugar evenly on the phylo sheet. Place a new phylo sheet on top of the first and press down evenly to flatten. Repeat this process until you have four layers.

Cut out circles with a ring cutter and place on a cookie sheet. Bake at 375° F until they are golden brown (about 10 minutes). Let them cool before plating.

To serve, spoon a circle of raspberry coulis on the plate, set a scoop of the parfait on it, and top with a phylo disc and fresh raspberries. Garnish with powdered sugar.

Walking into Muse is walking into another century. This Mediterranean restaurant draws its inspiration from the Villa of the Mysteries, a wine-producing estate found among the ruins of Pompeii. The sophisticated, celebratory culture of this lost civilization is told through its beautiful classical frescoes.

Owner Beth Anne Crane, a fourth-generation restaurateur, has created a space with traditional colors and hand-made majolica plates that is worthy of the ancient culture that inspires it. Rich reds, meandering frescoes, grape wall sconces and pillow-lined banquettes transport diners to a time when sharing food was a sacred ritual.

The menu centers on fruit of the sea, in keeping with its inspiration. Muse is also a wine bar with over 100 selections to choose from and enjoy by the glass. The candlelit setting includes a terrace for dining alfresco.

SIENNA RESTAURANT
CARAMEL SEMIFREDDO WITH DARK CHOCOLATE PRALINE FEUILLETINE & MILK CHOCOLATE GELATO

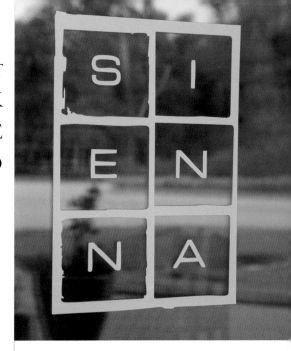

SERVES 6

CARAMEL SEMIFREDDO

3 cups heavy cream
1 2/3 cups sugar
water
18 large egg yolks

DARK CHOCOLATE PRALINE FEUILLETINE

6 ounces praline paste
3 ounces dark chocolate
4 ounces feuilletine

For MILK CHOCOLATE GELATO recipe,
See page 91

SAUCE

8 ounces sugar
water
7 ounces heavy cream

berries, to garnish

TO MAKE THE CARAMEL SEMIFREDDO, whip the cream until it forms soft peaks. Set aside in the refrigerator.

Put the sugar in a heavy saucepan and add just enough water to give the mixture the consistency of wet sand. Place over high heat and cook until it turns a light amber color.

Whip the egg yolks in an electric mixture with the wire whip attachment until pale yellow and light. Slowly pour the caramelized sugar into the yolks while beating at slow speed. Increase the speed to high and whip until the mixture is cool. Fold the whipped cream into the yolk mixture. Pour into 1 1/4-inch diameter molds and freeze. Any mold will work, or ramekins can be used and lined with parchment paper.

TO MAKE THE CHOCOLATE FEUILLETINE, combine the praline paste and dark chocolate in the top of a double boiler set over simmering water. Melt, stirring frequently, until smooth. Remove from the double boiler and let cool. Add feuilletine and mix it well.

Line a baking sheet with parchment paper. Spread the feuilletine mixture to a thickness of about 1/16 of an inch and freeze. When the mixture is solid, use a round 1 3/4-inch cookie cutter to cut out circles.

TO MAKE THE SAUCE, combine 8 ounces of sugar in a saucepan with enough water to make the sugar the texture of wet sand. Heat on high and stir until the sugar achieves an amber color. Remove from heat and stir in 7 ounces of heavy cream.

TO SERVE, place two chocolate praline rounds on each plate. Brush sauce in the middle of the plate. Unmold the semifreddo, and place on top of one of the chocolate rounds on each plate. Use two spoons to shape oval-shaped quenelles of the milk chocolate gelato and place one on the remaining chocolate praline round on each plate. Serve immediately.

This Daniel Island restaurant won Esquire's *Best New Restaurant in 2004 and the AAA Four Diamond Award in its first year and each year since. Chef Ken Vedrinski serves up innovative Italian cuisine in an upscale environment with vaulted ceilings and an open kitchen.*

Along with the restaurant honors, Esquire Magazine *also lauded Chef Ken as one of the Best Chefs in America. He created an organic vegetable garden behind the restaurant and now grows over 20 kinds of tomatoes, as well as herbs, fruits and even olives, for the restaurant. It allows him to serve ingredients that were plucked off the vine just moments before reaching the plate.*

Chef Ken grew up cooking alongside his grandmother, and has perfected his culinary art at the Four Seasons in Chicago and the Dining Room at Woodland's Resort. As Chef-owner of Sienna, he's an affable presence who enjoys engaging with patrons one on one.

BLOSSOM

RED VELVET BREAD PUDDING

What a colorful, lovely twist on bread pudding! The red velvet cake base adds new taste and texture, as well as festive color to an old favorite.

SERVES 8 TO 10

RED VELVET CAKE

1 cup unsalted butter, at room temperature
2 3/4 cups sugar
4 large eggs
1/2 cup red food color
2 1/2 teaspoons vanilla extract
6 tablespoons cocoa powder, sifted
2 teaspoons salt
2 cups buttermilk
3 1/2 cups all-purpose flour
2 1/2 teaspoons baking soda
2 1/2 teaspoons cider vinegar

BREAD PUDDING MIX

1 1/2 cups milk
1 1/2 cups heavy cream
2 large eggs
2 large egg yolks
3/4 cup sugar
Pinch of salt
6 ounces cream cheese, at room temperature
1 teaspoon vanilla extract

Strawberry or vanilla ice cream, to serve

Preheat the oven to 325° F. Line an 11-inch by 17-inch sheet pan with parchment paper.

TO MAKE THE CAKE, combine the butter and sugar in an electric mixer with a paddle attachment. Beat together until light and fluffy. Add the eggs, one at a time, beating until fully incorporated. Scrape down the bowl thoroughly and continue beating until the batter is completely smooth.

Mix together the food color, vanilla, cocoa powder, and salt in a small bowl. Sift it with the flour. Stir into the egg mixture. Add the buttermilk, alternating in three additions, scraping the bowl and paddle thoroughly. Combine the baking soda and the cider vinegar and mix into the batter. Spread evenly in the prepared pan.

Bake for about 30 minutes, until a tester inserted near the center of the cake comes out clean. Cool on a wire rack. When the cake is completely cool, cut into 1-inch cubes.

TO MAKE THE PUDDING MIX, combine the milk, cream, eggs, egg yolks, salt, and vanilla in a medium bowl.

Combine the cream cheese and sugar in a separate large bowl and beat together until smooth. Add 1/2 cup of the milk mixture to the cream cheese and mix until smooth. Mix in the remaining milk mixture.

Fill a large baking dish with the red velvet cake cubes. Add the cream cheese mixture, filling the baking dish to the top. Press all the cake cubes down into the pudding so that they are completely covered. Set the baking dish in a large pan and fill the large pan with enough warm water to reach halfway up the sides of the baking dish.

Bake for about 45 minutes, until the pudding is set.

Serve the bread pudding warm with ice cream.

This East Bay Street restaurant centers its menu on the abundant seafood of the region. Chef Donald Barickman of the Hospitality Management Group, oversees Blossom as the affordable, yet still upscale sister restaurant to Magnolia's next door.

Opened in 1993, it holds an Award of Excellence from Wine Spectator and is a favorite of young professionals. The atmosphere is airy with exposed white rafters, and sunlight coming through its many windows. There's an exhibition kitchen, and its energy adds to the convivial, upbeat setting.

The menu is Mediterranean-Charleston, with Low Country delicacies getting top billing here. A lush walled courtyard, with views of St. Philip's spire, offers an elegant space for dining alfresco.

LEMON PANNA COTTA WITH STRAWBERRIES AND VIN COTTO

SERVES 10

1 quart heavy cream
3/4 cup whole milk
Zest of 2 lemons
1/2 cup sugar
2 tablespoons honey
1/4 ounce packet unflavored gelatin
2 tablespoons water

2 pints strawberries, hulled and halved
1 tablespoon per serving, aged balsamic vinegar or vin cotto

sprigs of mint

Combine the cream, milk, lemon zest, sugar, and honey in a saucepan. Heat until small bubbles appear around the edge of the pan. Remove from the heat.

In a small bowl, sprinkle the gelatin over the water to soften. Let stand for 5 minutes. Add to the cream mixture while the mixture is still hot. Stir in the gelatin until completely dissolved. Let the mixture steep for at least 1 hour.

Strain the mixture through strainer into ten 6 1/2-ounce plastic ramekins. Leave the mixture ¼-inch from the rim. Refrigerate for 24 hours.

Combine the strawberries and balsamic vinegar in a bowl and let macerate for at least 10 minutes.

To SERVE, invert each ramekin onto a plate and poke a hole in bottom of the plastic cup. The panna cotta should pop out easily. Garnish each plate with the macerated strawberries and a sprig of mint.

This ultra-chic Italian ristorante opened in mid-2006, and has since won best new restaurant in Charleston by the City Paper. Restaurateur Hank Holliday took a City Market building with a history as biker bar, salsa club and burger joint, and has won Charleston's Historic Honor award for its transformation to upscale dining.

The amber lit interior has hues of warm Tuscan reds, a 1950s chandelier, leather booths and an illuminated staircase leading to the second level. To avoid the usual cacophony of bustling restaurants, fabric-coated sound installation panels have been installed in the ceiling.

Chef Jacques Larson, formerly of Cintra and Basil's Trattoria in Greensboro, North Carolina, cooks like an Italian who happens to live in the Low Country. He grew up with a love of "red food," and honed his culinary skills at the Mario-Batali owned Lupa in New York City and in restaurants across central and northern Italy.

MAGNOLIAS
SWEET BISCUITS WITH ORANGE CUSTARD SAUCE

SERVES 8

BISCUITS

7 tablespoons cold salted butter, diced
2 cups plus 2 tablespoons all-purpose White
   Lily flour
7 tablespoons sugar
1 tablespoon aluminum-free baking powder
3/4 teaspoon salt
1/2 cup buttermilk
2 tablespoons heavy cream

2 pints strawberries, hulled and sliced
2 tablespoons sugar

WHIPPED CREAM

1 cup heavy cream
1 1/2 tablespoons sugar
1/4 teaspoon vanilla extract

ORANGE CUSTARD SAUCE

2 cups heavy cream
1/2 cup sugar
Zest of 1/2 orange
1/4 vanilla bean, split lengthwise, or
   1/2 teaspoon vanilla extract
5 large egg yolks

Preheat the oven to 375° F.

TO MAKE THE BISCUITS, combine 2 cups flour, 3 tablespoons of the sugar, the baking powder, and salt in a mixing bowl. Add the diced butter and cut into the flour with a pastry cutter or two forks until the mixture is crumbly. Add the buttermilk, a little at a time, until the dough forms a ball. Place the dough on a floured surface, sprinkle it with the remaining 2 tablespoons flour, and pat it out to a 1-inch-thick circle. Cut the biscuits with a 2 1/2-inch biscuit cutter and place them on a baking sheet. Brush the tops of the biscuits with cream and sprinkle generously with the remaining 4 tablespoons sugar.

Bake for 15 to 20 minutes, until golden. Remove the biscuits from the oven, cool to room temperature.

TO MAKE THE CUSTARD SAUCE, combine the cream with 1/4 cup of the sugar, the orange zest, and the vanilla bean, if using, in a heavy-bottomed saucepan over medium heat. Cook until there are small bubbles around the edges.

In a separate bowl, beat the egg yolks with the remaining 1/4 cup sugar until well blended. Very slowly pour the hot cream into the egg yolk mixture, stirring constantly. When half of the cream is incorporated into the egg mixture, slowly pour the mixture back into the pan of hot cream, stirring continuously.

Place the pan over low heat and, stirring constantly with a wooden spoon, cook the custard until it is thick enough to coat the back of the spoon. Strain into a metal bowl. Scrape the beans from the vanilla pod into the custard. Discard the vanilla bean and the orange zest. If you are using vanilla extract, add that now. Cool immediately by placing the bowl in a larger bowl that has been filled with ice, stirring occasionally. Cover and refrigerate. The sauce will keep in the refrigerator for 2 to 3 days.

TO PREPARE THE STRAWBERRIES, toss the berries with the sugar and let sit for 5 minutes. The combination of the sugars and the natural juices of the strawberries will produce a simple strawberry syrup.

TO MAKE THE WHIPPED CREAM, pour the cold cream into a chilled mixing bowl. Begin beating, slowly adding in the sugar and vanilla. Continue to beat until the cream has tripled in volume and is firm, yet creamy.

TO SERVE, split the biscuits in half horizontally and spoon the strawberries over the bottom halves, add a dollop of whipped cream to each, and replace the tops. Spoon on the custard sauce as desired, and serve.

Magnolia's is situated in the circa 1739 former Customs House on the oldest street in Charleston. Opened in 1990, it's been a longtime favorite in Charleston, and still a place to see and be seen in the historic district.

The interior has heart-pine floors with wrought iron accents, and specially commissioned paintings by Taos artist Ron Goebel. Southern Living magazine has called Magnolia's the most celebrated in Charleston, for its traditional Low Country fare done with an innovative flair. Pastry chef Katie Gulla oversees pastry, pasta and bread production at Magnolia's and Blossom, and supports the Susan G. Komen Breast Cancer Foundation in her free time with her culinary skills.

Magnolia's has been given the Fodors Choice and Wine Spectator Award of Excellence. It's also been a member of DiRONA since 1995. Owner-chef Donald Barickman and Chef Don Drake work together to create consistently good regional favorites. Chef Drake trained with Roy Yamaguchi of Roy's in Honolulu, among others.

This classic dessert has been on the Magnolia menu since the restaurant opened 20 years ago. It is the Southern twist on strawberry shortcake.

PECAN-INFUSED TIRAMISÙ

SERVES 15

1 handful pecans, toasted
2/3 cups milk
1/4 cup cognac
1 (1/2-ounce) packets plain gelatin
1 tablespoons water
3 large egg yolks, beaten
1 1/4 cups sugar

1 (16-ounce) container mascarpone
1 2/3 cups heavy cream
3 large egg whites
1/2 tablespoon vanilla sugar (see Note)
1/2 pinch cream of tartar

Combine pecans, milk, and cognac in a saucepan and bring to a boil. Remove from the heat and let steep for 1 to 2 hours.

Sprinkle the gelatin over the water in a small bowl. Let soften for 5 minutes.

Transfer the pecan mixture to the top of a double boiler set over simmering water. Add the egg yolks, sugar, and gelatin, whisking until smooth. Heat just until warm.

Remove from the heat and whisk in the mascarpone.

Beat the heavy cream until soft peaks form. Fold into the mascarpone mixture.

In a clean, dry bowl, whip the egg whites until foamy. Add the vanilla sugar and cream of tartar and continue to whip until the mixture forms soft peaks. Fold into the mascarpone mixture.

Spoon into 6-ounce martini glasses, chill in the refrigerator. Serve cold.

NOTE: To make vanilla sugar, combine 1 cup granulated white sugar and 1 whole vanilla bean in an airtight container and store at room temperature, shaking the jar occasionally. The sugar will be infused with vanilla flavor in 1 to 2 weeks, and it will keep indefinitely.

Charleston Grill has risen to prominence via its nationally lauded chef Bob Waggoner. He perfected his art in Michelin-rated restaurants across France, and in 1988, became the first American to own and Chef his own establishment there. Waggoner is an acknowledged master, granted an honorary doctorate from Johnson and Wales University, and in another first, knighted by the French government.

At the Charleston Grill he fuses Low Country cooking with French culinary traditions. Chef Waggoner's menu has four sections – Southern, Pure, Lush and Cosmopolitan. Diners can choose from simple to extravagant, regional to world cuisine, or sample some of each. Chef Waggoner's cuisine combines unusual ingredients and classic techniques, which he's shared as a cooking expert on countless shows, including "Gourmet Getaways with Robin Leach," and segments airing on CNN, The Travel Channel and PBS.

Situated in the historic district's Charleston Place hotel, Charleston Grill is a pinnacle of fine dining with dark mahogany woodwork and green marble floors that seem rooted in tradition and elegance.

CHARLESTON GRILL

White Chocolate Pear Bread Pudding

SERVES 10

BREAD PUDDING

4 cups heavy cream

2 cups milk

2 1/2 cups raw sugar, or brown sugar

8 ounces white couverture

24 sugared yolks

12 croissants, chopped

3 pears, peeled, cored, and chopped

CARAMEL SAUCE

2 1/2 cups raw sugar, or brown sugar

3/4 teaspoon fresh lemon juice

Water, as needed

3/4 cup heavy cream

1 cup butter, cubed

3/4 teaspoon vanilla extract

Preheat the oven to 350° F.

To MAKE THE PUDDING, bring the cream, milk, and sugar to a boil in a large saucepan.

Put the couverture in one bowl. Put the sugared yolks in a separate bowl.

When the cream mixture comes to a boil, pour over the couverture and whisk until smooth. Pour the couverture mixture over the sugared yolks and whisk until smooth. Add the croissants and chopped pears and toss to soak and coat. Divide among 10 ovenproof 6-ounce bowls.

Bake 30 to 45 minutes, until light brown and springy to the touch.

To MAKE THE CARAMEL SAUCE, combine the sugar and lemon juice in a heavy saucepan. Add just enough water to give the mixture the consistency of wet sand. Cook, stirring, until the sugar caramelizes to a dark caramel color. Add the cream, butter, and vanilla, taking care to avoid the resulting steam. Whisk until smooth.

Place in an ice bath to cool, stirring occasionally.

Serve the hot bread pudding with the cold caramel sauce drizzled on top.

ICE CREAM, GELATO, COOKIES & SAUCES

A coastal town blessed with numerous beautiful bays, beaches, marshes and creeks, Charlestonians enjoys summertime, and our warm-weather treat of choice is, naturally, ice cream. Most recently, however, ice cream has been turning up year-round on menus throughout the city.

These ice cream recipes range from the simple, wholesome flavors of Wholly Cow creamery to the fine dining concoctions of Tristan's Chilled Blueberry Soup.

The Wentworth Grill's Coffee and Donuts ice cream is a playfully tasty dish that makes me giggle like a kid. That must be the reason we love ice cream so much—it never fails to bring back memories of childhood: sunny beaches, the hum of ceiling fans, and the tinkle of the ice cream truck coming up the street.

As the simple name suggests, Fish presents local, sustainable seafood in an Eastern minimalist style that retains its true, natural flavor.

Owners Charles and Celeste Patrick painstakingly restored the circa 1837 Charleston home, along with the William Aiken House and The American Theatre, bringing new life to the N. King Street area. Care was taken to retain traditional elements, like the pillars outside and pistils, while updating it for fine dining.

Fish opened in 2000 with Executive Chef Nico Romo at the helm in the kitchen. Romo brings French techniques from his native Lyon, with an innovative style honed over many years in elite culinary kitchens.

His career took him to Chez Phillippe in the Peabody Hotel, the Café at the Ritz Carlton in Atlanta, and the Café at East Andrews, the post from which he was guest Chef for his third James Beard dinner. Romo recently opened the third location of B.E.D. restaurant concepts for the first Atlanta luxury boutique, the Glenn.

FISH RESTAURANT
ANCHOR PORTER ICE CREAM SANDWICHES

SERVES 10

OATMEAL COOKIES

3 cups old-fashioned rolled oats
1 1/4 cups all-purpose flour
1/2 teaspoon baking powder
1/2 teaspoon baking soda
Pinch of salt
3/4 cup unsalted butter, melted
2 tablespoons vegetable oil
1 cup granulated white sugar
1 cup firmly packed light brown sugar
2 large eggs
1 cup dried cherries, chopped
1 cup chocolate chips

ANCHOR PORTER ICE CREAM

1 (12-ounce) bottle Anchor Porter beer, at room temperature
2 1/4 cups heavy cream
2 1/4 cups half-and-half
1 tablespoon instant espresso powder
6 large egg yolks
1 cup firmly packed brown sugar
1/4 cup molasses
1/2 cup finely chopped good-quality bittersweet chocolate
1/4 cup crystallized ginger, finely chopped

Preheat the oven to 350° F. Line two large baking sheets with parchment paper.

To make the oatmeal cookies, whisk together the oats, flour, baking powder, and salt in a large bowl.

Combine the butter, oil, white and brown sugars, and eggs in a separate bowl. Beat until smooth. Add the oat mixture and stir until well-blended. Fold in the cherries and chocolate chips. Using an ice cream scoop, scoop balls of dough onto the cookie sheets, leaving about 2 inches of space between cookies.

Bake for about 15 minutes, until golden brown Transfer to a wire rack to cool.

To make the ice cream, set out two bowls, one slightly smaller than the other, but still large enough to hold all 2 quarts of the custard. Fill the larger bowl with ice cubes and little bit of cold water. Place the smaller bowl into ice bowl. Finally, into this smaller bowl, place a strainer.

In a small saucepan, heat the beer to just barely simmering. Leave it on the stove to keep warm.

In separate saucepan, bring the heavy cream, half-and-half, and espresso powder to a boil.

While the cream mixture heats, whisk together the egg yolks, brown sugar, and molasses in a medium bowl. When the cream mixture has come to a boil, remove it from the heat. Whisk a couple of tablespoons of the hot cream mixture into the egg mixture. Continue whisking in small amounts of hot cream until both mixtures are at roughly the same temperature. You should see a little bit of steam coming off both. Pour all of the egg mixture into the cream mixture and add the beer.

Cook the custard mixture over medium-high heat, stirring constantly with a wooden spoon, until the custard has thickened enough to coat the back of the spoon. If you run your finger down the back of the spoon it should leave a trail. The mixture should read 170° F on a thermometer.

Pour the custard into the strainer in the bowl set over the ice. Allow the mixture to cool, stirring occasionally.

When the mixture is very cold, pour into an ice-cream maker and freeze according to the manufacturer's directions.

When the ice cream is frozen, fold in the chocolate and ginger. Transfer to an airtight container and let the ice cream harden in the freezer for several hours before serving. This recipe makes two quarts.

To SERVE, place one scoop of ice cream between two cookies.

Dublin-born Chef Ciaran Duffy is a gregarious showman, and even wears a Chef Cam that's broadcasted on the Tristan website. He's been show-cased at the James Beard House in New York and took part in the World Culinary Olympics in 2000 as sous chef, with the team winning third place. He's even appeared on Wheel of Fortune, when the show taped a Charleston segment.

Chef Duffy's cuisine is constantly evolving, and he integrates what he learns while doing stints at places like The Fat Duck in London. He's not afraid to experiment with flavors, and his choco-late BBQ sauce is now sold in gourmet shops. The open kitchen at Tristan reminds diners that an artist is hard at work, one whose adventurous choices make him stand out.

The décor is sleek metropolitan, with a water wall in the bar, glass artwork and high-style terrace for dining alfresco. Such ambiance, along with the cre-ative force of Chef Duffy, makes Tristan a dining experience with few rivals.

TRISTAN
CHILLED BLUEBERRY SOUP

SERVES 5

BLUEBERRY SOUP

3 cups pureed blueberries
1 cup water
1/2 cup granulated white sugar
2 tablespoons fresh lemon juice
1/2 teaspoon ground coriander
Pinch of ground cinnamon
Pinch of ground cloves
2 tablespoons red wine
2/3 cup plain yogurt
2/3 cup sour cream

BUTTERMILK VANILLA ICE CREAM

3 cups heavy cream
1 1/2 cups granulated sugar
1 vanilla bean
15 large egg yolks, beaten
2 cups buttermilk

CORNMEAL SHORTBREAD COOKIES

1 2/3 cups all-purpose flour
2 tablespoons cornmeal
3 1/2 tablespoons granulated white sugar
1 1/2 tablespoons baking powder
1/8 teaspoon salt
6 tablespoons unsalted butter
2/3 cup plus 1 tablespoon heavy cream
1 tablespoon turbinado sugar

TO MAKE THE BLUEBERRY SOUP, combine the blueberry puree, water, white sugar, lemon juice, co-riander, cinnamon, and cloves in a saucepan. Bring to a boil, stirring, to dissolve sugar. Remove the pan from the heat and set in a bowl of ice to chill, stirring occasionally.

Stir in the red wine, yogurt, and sour cream. Refrigerate.

Preheat the oven to 350° F.

TO MAKE THE COOKIES, combine the flour, cornmeal, sugar, baking powder, and salt in a food processor. Pulse to mix. Add the butter and pulse until it is a coarse meal. Transfer into a bowl and mix in the 2/3 cup cream with clean hands. Do not overmix!

Roll out on a lightly floured surface to a thickness of 1 inch. Cut into 3-inch rounds with a cookie cutter. Brush the tops of the cookies with the remaining tablespoon of cream and sprinkle with turbinado sugar. Transfer to a baking sheet.

Bake approximately 10 to 12 minutes, or until golden brown. Cool on wire racks.

TO MAKE THE ICE CREAM, combine the cream and 3/4 cup white sugar in a saucepan. Split the vanilla bean and scrape the seeds into the mixture. Add the bean as well. Bring just to a boil. Spoon a little of the hot cream mixture into the egg yolks and mix well. Continue adding a little cream until the egg yolks are warm. Pour all the egg yolks into the cream mixture. Return to the heat and cook, stirring, until the custard thickens and coats the back of a spoon.

Place the saucepan in a bowl of ice and let cool, stirring occasionally. Discard the vanilla bean. Stir in the buttermilk. Freeze in an ice-cream maker according to the manufacturer's directions.

TO SERVE, cut a warm biscuit in half and put a scoop of buttermilk vanilla ice cream inside. Top with the other half and pour soup around the biscuit.

WENTWORTH GRILL
COFFEE AND DONUTS

A good cook knows how to use leftovers, and Chef John Therres says that the hotel always has left-over coffee and doughnuts from their breakfast buffet. He shows a great sense of fun with this surprising twist on a breakfast combo.

Located inside the Renaissance Hotel in downtown Charleston, the Wentworth Grill serves Lowcountry favorites with notable originality. There are white tablecloths and French doors leading out onto Wentworth Street, in this AAA Four Diamond rated restaurant.

Part of the Marriot chain, it's one of the first to offer trans-fat free cuisine in the area. Signature dishes of Chef John Therres include Hickory Smoked Pork Chop and Jumbo Lump Crabcake.

Local food critics called it a surprise despite its unassuming décor. It won Best Hotel in a Restaurant by the Charleston City Paper in 2006. And the bartender Henry Fincke brought Wentworth Grill notoriety by concocting the official drink for ChazzFest 2007—it's called the Chazz Julep.

The desserts here are well worth the visit, and, other than this one, try the extravagant Rum and Coca-cola Cake Trifle.

SERVES 4

ICE CREAM

8 Krispy Kreme glazed doughnuts, stale
4 cups heavy cream
1 vanilla bean
1 cup half-and-half
2 large egg yolks
1 tablespoon granulated white sugar
1/2 teaspoon salt

HOT FUDGE

11/4 cups granulated white sugar
1/2 cup firmly packed light brown sugar
1/2 cup unsweetened cocoa powder
2 tablespoons all-purpose flour
1/4 cup unsalted butter
3/4 cup brewed coffee
1/4 teaspoon salt

RASPBERRY WHIPPED CREAM

1 cup whipping cream
About 1/4 cup raspberry preserves

TO MAKE THE ICE CREAM, process the doughnut in a food processor until small and crumbly. Blend with heavy cream. Halve the vanilla bean, scrape seeds out, and add both seeds and pod to the cream mixture. Let steep for 2 hours.

Meanwhile, scald the half-and-half in the top of a double boiler over simmering water..

Beat the yolks with the sugar and salt in a separate bowl. Slowly whisk in some of the half-and-half until both mixtures are the same temperature. Heat over a double-boiler until thickened, 3 to 4 minutes. Let cool completely. Blend the half-and-half mixture with salt and doughnut mixture and strain through a large strainer (do not use a fine strainer). Chill for 1 hour.

When the custard is cold, freeze in an ice-cream maker according to the manufacturer's directions. The ice cream can be formed into doughnut shapes by hand before the ice cream is fully frozen, and then returned to your freezer to set, if you want to serve the dessert as shown.

TO MAKE THE HOT FUDGE, whisk together the white sugar, brown sugar, cocoa powder, and flour in a saucepan. Add the butter, coffee, and salt. Heat gently until somewhat thickened, about 5 minutes. The sauce will continue to thicken after it is removed from the heat.

TO MAKE THE RASPBERRY WHIPPED CREAM, combine the whipping cream and preserves in a bowl and beat until soft peaks form.

TO SERVE, place two scoops of ice cream, or two ice cream doughnut on a plate, slather with hot fudge, and finish with a dollop of the raspberry whipped cream.

WHOLLY COW
KILLA VANILLA

This is Wholly Cow's biggest-selling flavor for the last 23 years. They've got it just right!

SERVES 8 (1/2 CUP SERVINGS)

2 cups half-and-half
1 cup whipping cream
1 cup sugar
2 large egg yolks
1 vanilla bean, split and scraped

Combine the half-and-half, whipping cream, sugar, egg yolks, and vanilla seeds and pod in a large saucepan and place over medium heat. Cook, stirring constantly, until the mixture reaches 180° F. You will need an accurate thermometer for this step. Do not guess at the temperature.

Once properly heated, immediately remove from the heat. Discard the vanilla bean pod (save for a later date) and let the mixture cool to room temperature. Refrigerate. The mix is the best if it can age overnight before use.

Freeze in an ice-cream maker according to the manufacturer's directions. Electric ice-cream makers will generally do a better job of freezing than hand churns and make for a smoother mouth feel.

Any ice cream should be consumed within 24 hours of freezing for the best flavor and consistency.

NOTES: *For a more custard flavor, add another egg yolk. To increase the sweetness, add some brown sugar (1 teaspoon). If you don't have a vanilla bean, use 1 tablespoon of Nielsen Massey bourbon vanilla. (It is the best vanilla extract.) Cheap vanilla and artificial vanillin will ruin the flavor of the ice cream; don't do it!*

Now sold all over South Carolina, Wholly Cow started in 1985 as the vision of Rob and Laurie Kramer, to create the best tasting ice cream in the state. There are store franchises now that sell both frozen goodies and coffee, and you can find Wholly Cow in its packaged form.

Theirs is high-density ice cream used in many regional fine dining establishments. Wholly Cow has an ultra-rich 16 % butterfat content, which gives it a creamy texture. They also process it to minimize air content, so that each pint weights much more than an actual pint. Of course, Wholly Cow ice cream has secret ingredients, too, that have been refined in the past two decades.

The Kramers base their business on honesty and integrity, and providing all-natural ice cream products and locally roasted coffee. They've got 18 flavors, including three that are sugar free, along with sorbets and sherbets. And they introduce seasonal flavors, like the summer favorite "Hunka Hunka Banana Love," with peanut butter cups and chocolate chips.

39 Rue De Jean
Vacherin

This is a version of a traditional French dessert, consisting of meringue rings stacked on one another, with a pastry or meringue base. The rings are then filled with chantilly cream and/or ice cream and seasonal fruit.

SERVES 8

MERINGUES

10 large egg whites, at room temperature
3/4 cup granulated white sugar
Pinch of cream of tartar

FILLING

1 pint vanilla bean ice cream
1 pint raspberry sorbet

WHIPPED CREAM

3 cups heavy whipping cream
1 1/4 cups confectioners' sugar

2 cups toasted sliced blanched almonds, crushed by hand

TO MAKE THE MERINGUES, whip the egg whites until foamy in an electric mixer fitted with the wire whip attachment on high speed. Decrease to medium speed and pour in in the sugar and cream of tartar in a slow steady stream. Return the mixer to high speed and whip until stiff peaks form

Preheat the oven to 225° F.

Cover a large flat baking sheet with parchment paper and trace at least sixteen 3 3/4-inch diameter circles as a template for the meringues (a large coffee cup works well for this). Fit a 10-inch pastry bag with a large round tip. Transfer the meringue into the bag and pipe into the circles, working from the outside in. The meringues should be about 1/3 inch thick.

Bake the meringues until dry. This can take 24 to 36 hours, depending on the humidity. Meringues are done when they are crispy all the way through. It's always a good idea to pipe out a few extra in the previous step for testing at this stage.

When the meringues are crispy, allow to cool briefly. If you are not going to use the meringues immediately, store them in an airtight container, and they will normally stay crisp for 2 to 3 days. If they do get soft or tacky, you can return them to the oven for an hour or so, and this will solve the problem.

TO ASSEMBLE THE DESSERT, place eight meringues with the flat side down on a tray that will fit in the freezer, allowing about 1 inch of space between each. Using a 1 1/2-ounce scoop, drop one scoop of vanilla ice cream onto each meringue. Drop one scoop of raspberry sorbet on top of the ice cream. Place the other 8 meringues on top of the sorbet with the flat side of the meringue up. Using the palm of your hand, press down evenly and lightly, until dessert is about 3 1/2 inches high, without letting the ice cream or sorbet come over the sides. It's helpful to allow the ice cream and sorbet to thaw slightly at this point. Once assembled, place the tray in the freezer for 2 hours for the ice cream and sorbet to set.

Once the vacherins are set, whip cream and confectioners' sugar to medium stiff peaks. Remove the vacherins from the freezer and ice each individually with the whipped cream using a cake knife or spatula, spreading the whipped cream on the sides first, then the top. Return to the freezer for 1 hour.

Known by locals simply as "Rue," this classic brasserie takes its name from its location on 39 John Street in the historic district. With its traditional French zinc bar, pommes frites and often boisterous patrons, 39 Rue de Jean brings the atmosphere of the Left Bank to Charleston's Francophiles.

After a visit to 39 Rue de Jean, you'll know why it's voted Best French every year by the Charleston City Paper since opening in 2001. It's housed in a 2-story brick historic building that dates to 1880, but was re-designed in 1943, in the Art Moderne style of the time.

A popular place to see and be seen, this lively scene goes on well into the evening.

Remove the vacherins from the freezer and allow the whipped cream to thaw slightly on the outside, 5 to 10 minutes. Place the crushed almonds in a metal mixing bowl and gently roll each vacherin in the almonds. Return the vacherins to the tray and freeze until you are ready for them.

It is best to allow the vacherins to thaw slightly (about 5 minutes) before serving.

NOTE: You can garnish the dessert with whipped cream and fresh raspberries or strawberries. If you feel a sauce is in order, a raspberry coulis or crème anglaise both work well.

Smoked Honey Vanilla Ice Cream, Carolina's

MAKES 1 QUART

1 cup whole milk	2/3 cups sugar
1 cup heavy cream	1 teaspoon vanilla extract
1/4 vanilla bean	2 tablespoons smoked honey
5 large egg yolks	(available online)

Combine the milk and cream in a heavy saucepan. Cut the vanilla bean in half lengthwise and scrape the seeds into the mixture. Add the pod also. Bring almost to a boil.

In another bowl, beat the egg yolks with the sugar until well combined. Slowly pour a little of the hot milk mixture into the yolks. Continue to whisk in small amounts of the milk mixture at a time, until the temperatures of the two mixtures are equal. Whisk all of the yolk into the remaining milk mixture..

Cook over medium heat, stirring, until the mixture has thickened and will coat the back of the spoon. Stir in the vanilla extract mixture and 2 tablespoons smoked honey. Strain the mixture into a bowl, discarding the vanilla bean. Place the bowl in a larger bowl of ice and let cool, stirring occasionally.

Transfer to an ice-cream maker and freeze according to the manufacturer's directions.

Cinnamon-Rosemary Ice Cream, Cordavi

MAKES 2 QUARTS

2 cups heavy cream	Couple sprigs of rosemary
2 cups milk	1/2 vanilla bean
2 tablespoons corn syrup	10 large egg yolks
Pinch of salt	1 cup sugar

Combine the cream, milk, corn syrup, salt, cinnamon, vanilla bean, and rosemary in a pan. Bring to a simmer and turn off the heat. Let the vanilla and rosemary steep in the milk for another 10 to 15 minutes, to taste. Remove the vanilla and rosemary.

Whisk yolks and sugar together until combined. Slowly stir the warm cream mixture into the yolks, whisking constantly. Pour back into the pan and cook over low heat, stirring constantly, until the mixture is thickened and coats the back of a spoon. Transfer the mixture to a bowl and set the bowl in a larger bowl of ice. Let cool, stirring occasionally.

MILK CHOCOLATE GELATO, SIENNA

3 cups heavy cream
1 cup whole milk
1 1/4 cups sugar
3 tablespoons honey
4 ounces milk chocolate
14 large egg yolks

Combine the cream, milk, sugar, and honey in a heavy saucepan. Bring almost to a boil.

In another bowl, beat the egg yolks until well combined. Slowly pour a little of the hot cream mixture into the yolks. Continue to whisk in small amounts of milk at a time until the temperatures of the two mixtures are equal. Whisk all of the yolk mixture into the cream mixture. Cook over medium heat, stirring, until the mixture has thickened and will coat the back of the spoon.

Put the milk chocolate in a bowl. Whisk the hot custard into the milk chocolate until smooth. Place the bowl in a larger bowl of ice and let cool, stirring occasionally.

Transfer to an ice-cream maker and freeze according to the manufacturer's directions.

PRALINES, ANSON
MAKES 8

1 cup granulated white sugar
1/4 cup firmly packed brown sugar
1/2 cup buttermilk
1/2 teaspoon baking soda
2 tablespoons unsalted butter
1 cup pecans, lightly toasted
1/2 teaspoon vanilla extract

Line a cookie sheet with greased parchment paper, waxed paper, or a silicone liner.

TO MAKE THE PRALINES, combine the white and brown sugars, buttermilk, and baking soda in a small saucepan over low heat. Cook, stirring constantly, until the sugars are dissolved. Add the butter and increase the heat to a medium-high. Bring to a boil, without stirring, and continue to boil until the mixture reaches 236° F on an accurate candy thermometer.

Remove from the heat and stir in the pecans and the vanilla. Mix with a wooden spoon until the praline mixture becomes opaque. With a regular tablespoon, scoop up a little of the praline and, with the back of a second spoon, scrape the praline off, and drop onto the prepared cookie sheet. Cool for 30 minutes. (The pralines may be made in advance and stored airtight for up to 72 hours, but no more, before serving.)

Cocoa Sauce, Kiawah Resort

SERVES 12

1 cup cocoa	Pinch of salt
1 cup sugar	1 cup water

Combine the cocoa, sugar, and salt in a small saucepan. Slowly stir in the water. Bring to a boil, decrease the heat, and allow to simmer for a few minutes until it has thickened. Strain into a container and refrigerate.

Caramel Sauce, Sienna

8 ounces sugar
water (enough to make sugar
 like wet sand)
7 ounces heave cream

Combine 8 ounces of sugar in a saucepan with enough water to make the sugar the texture of wet sand. Heat on high and stir until the sugar achieves an amber color. Remove from heat and stir in 7 ounces of heavy cream.

Cornmeal Cookies, Circa 1886

MAKES 3 DOZEN

3/4 cup unsalted butter, at room temperature	1 tablespoon honey
2/3 cup sugar, plus more for sprinkling	2 large egg yolks
1/4 teaspoon salt	zest of 1 orange, finely grated
1/2 teaspoon vanilla extract	1 cup white bread flour
	1 cup yellow cornmeal

Beat together the butter, 2/3 cup sugar, and salt until light and fluffy. Beat in the vanilla, honey, egg yolks, and orange zest. Add the bread flour and cornmeal and mix until well combined. Remove from the bowl, shape into a disk, and wrap in plastic wrap. Chill for at least 1 hour.

Preheat the oven to 350° F.

Roll out cookies on a lightly floured to surface to a thickness of 1/4 inch. Cut out with any desired cookie cutter. Sprinkle with sugar. Transfer to a large baking sheet.

Bake the cookies for 8 to 10 minutes, until golden brown.

Transfer to wire racks to cool.

Coconut Caramel Sauce, Palmetto Cafe

SERVES 6

1 cup heavy cream
1 (13.5-ounce) can coconut milk
1 (15-ounce) can Coco Lopez
cream of coconut

2 cups firmly packed brown sugar
4 cups sweetened shredded
coconut

Combine the heavy cream, coconut milk, cream of coconut, brown sugar, and coconut in a heavy saucepan. Bring to a boil and boil gently for 25 minutes, or until thick, stirring frequently. Set aside and let cool.

Caramel Parfait, Cypress

1 1/4 cups granulated white sugar
Water
3 cups heavy cream
5 tablespoons milk

1/2 vanilla bean, split and scraped
8 large egg yolks
1 large egg white

Put 1 cup of the white sugar in a heavy saucepan. Add enough water to create a consistency of wet sand. Be sure there are no dry pockets of sugar. If necessary, wet down the sides of the pot with a pastry brush to remove any sugar crystals. Cook the sugar over high heat, undisturbed, until it begins to color around the edges of the pot. Swirl the sugar to evenly distribute the heat. Caramelize the sugar until very, very dark and foam forms on top of the sugar, then begins to dissipate. (Caution: Be very careful because this hot caramelized sugar will stick to the skin, resulting in painful burns.)

As soon as the sugar reaches the desired color, carefully pour in the cream. Reduce the heat to medium and whisk slowly until the sugar has melted and the mixture is smooth. Strain and chill the caramel cream overnight.

The next day, in an electric mixer fitted with a whip attachment, whip the cold caramel cream to medium stiffness. Remove from the bowl and store in the refrigerator until needed.

Combine the milk, the remaining 1/4 cup white sugar, split vanilla bean and seeds, egg yolks, and egg white in a stainless steel saucepan over medium heat. Whisk the mixture continuously until the mixture appears foamy and thick. Continue to cook to a temperature of 165° F. Do not overcook or you will curdle the eggs.

Immediately pour the custard through a fine strainer into the bowl of an electric mixer. Using the whisk attachment, whip the custard on high until the bowl feels cooler than body temperature.

In a large bowl, gently whisk the whipped, cooled custard into the caramel whipped cream. Wrap the bowl and freeze overnight.

INDEX

Much of the credit for this book goes, along with my heartfelt thanks, to Marion Sullivan, whose informed guidance helped shape it. Her willingness to share her wealth of knowledge and her love of the city and its food is a great tribute to Charleston.

I could not have completed this book without the happy assistance of my friend and colleague, Angela Rojas. Thanks also for the research and editorial help of Andrea Chesman, Molly Hall Nagy, Joanna Brodmann, and Judie Arvites.

Many thanks to Dr. Calhoun and Nina Kooij at Pelican Publishing Company for their encouragement, help and support.

And finally, I'm grateful to my friend, Deborah Whitlaw Llewellyn, for her wonderful photography and for her willingness to share a dozen desserts a day with me while we were shooting. You are the best, Deborah!